GOYA

GOYA

JEAN-FRANÇOIS CHABRUN

LONDON
THAMES AND HUDSON

TRANSLATED FROM THE FRENCH
BY J. MAXWELL BROWNJOHN

Contents

PART THREE: CHAOS, SOLITUDE AND GLORY (1808-1828)

PART ONE:

OBSCURITY (1746-1792)

A village in Aragón

The mule-path leading from Zaragoza to Fuendetodos is still as muddy or rutted, according to place and time of year, as it was in the days when Francisco Goya trotted along it with the unflagging energy of a headstrong child. Several miles from the Aragonese capital the white cottages of the village still cluster round the wind-swept belfry. The red and yellow ochre mountains still stand silhouetted against the blue of the sky, and no changes have been made in the house inhabited by the Goya family when Francisco first saw the light of day on 30 March 1746, in the reign of Philip V.

A low, dark doorway leads directly off the narrow street into a sunken kitchen, an old-style room dominated by an immense fireplace. In front of the fireplace stand two stone benches which were presumably spread with animal hides on winter evenings to provide a warm

GOYA'S BIRTHPLACE AT FUENDETODOS

sleeping-place. Eugenio d'Ors tells us that he spent a long time there before embarking on his *Life of Goya*: 'Like an eskimo's igloo, the kitchen has no aperture but its chimney. The wood that burns there disperses not only its heat but a good part of its smoke and almost all the delightful fragrance of evaporating resin between the rough walls and low ceiling, which might have been hewn out of a cave. If a bunch of rosemary is kept there it will scent the confined air for more than a month. If fat melts in the hearth it impregnates stone, brick, furniture, tongue - even hands . . . '

'Savouring the inertia, the oblivion, the *prehistory* of the place, like someone savouring a hot bread soup', Eugenio d'Ors stood lost in thought before the trough 'where Goya's mother with her rough hands and rolled-up sleeves must have panted as she kneaded the good flour that stilled her child's hunger'.

'But this hunger', the writer goes on, 'was such that the family's bread could not assuage it for long. And so, breaking away, the child went off to rend the world with his wolfish teeth and devour it like a one-pound loaf'.

In fact, Francisco never dreamed of 'devouring the world like a one-pound loaf', neither at Fuendetodos nor in Zaragoza, where he settled with his family when he was about fourteen, nor in Madrid, where he arrived at the age of eighteen. Instead, he was content to cut off a slice and eat it with the resigned dignity that characterizes a Spanish peasant of good stock.

'A race like a vine, scorched by sun and tanned by frosts; a sober race, the product of a long selective process governed by the cold of harsh winters and by periodic famines; a race inured to inclement skies and a life of deprivation. The Spanish peasant is serene in his gestures, poised and grave in his conversation, reminiscent of a dethroned monarch...'

Miguel de Unamuno's description probably applies more closely to the *batturo,* or Aragonese peasant, than to any other, and Francisco Goya, the dethroned monarch, was one such.

His father, José Goya, was not exactly a peasant. The son of a notary and a gilder by trade, he was prompted by lack of success to interrupt his professional activities and cultivate a few acres of land at Fuendetodos in order to feed his daughter and three sons until they were of an age to earn their own living.

Tending goats and pigs in all weathers, carrying heavy two-handled tubs of precious water in glaring sunlight or icy winds, rambling through the countryside, sling in hand – such were the childhood activities of the four Goya children: Rita, the daughter, Tomás, who was training to be a gilder like his father, Camillo, destined for the priesthood, and Francisco, the painter-to-be. There seems little reason why, when he resumed work as a master-gilder at 12 Calle de la Moreria, Zaragoza, in about 1760, José Goya should have been averse to the idea that his son Francisco wanted to become a painter. Painting was not an 'artistic' profession at this period, but a skilled trade like any other. It was no more socially discreditable to gild church retables or the panelled walls of country houses than it was to measure the extent of a property on behalf of a notary. The only difference between a painter and a gilder or surveyor was that the painter was allowed to put something on the interior of premises (pious allegories in churches and genre scenes in country houses) and that, instead of measuring land, he reproduced as faithfully as he could the physiognomy of those who owned it.

Goya's mother was a realist. When he left for Madrid she slipped into his pocket a small notebook in which she had carefully recorded the genealogies of prominent families, especially those of Aragonese origin. This notebook was to be her son's order book. It contained the names of all the people who in our day would have attracted the attention of a budding society photographer anxious to sell pictures of personalities in the public eye to popular magazines.

The existence of this little notebook proves that Francisco de Goya y Lucientes had big ideas when he embarked on his career. He aimed to become a 'painter of the great' and does not seem to have been over-awed by the fame of his first master, José de Lujan y Martinez.

Lujan was not a negligible figure at this period. A court painter at the age of thirty, he had studied in Naples and painted with extreme meticulousness in the syrupy and stereotyped style which Italy had imposed upon the whole of Europe for almost a century. In Zaragoza, where Lujan lived in affluence, he commanded universal respect. The Inquisition greatly esteemed his talent for adding drapery to medieval or Renaissance paintings so as to conceal the expanses of flesh that sprawled shame-

VIEW OF ZARAGOZA AT THE BEGINNING OF THE EIGHTEENTH CENTURY

lessly across them. His official designation was 'Reviser of Indecent Paintings', but he was a good man who did not hesitate to take penniless pupils into his atelier for the sake of art.

What did he teach them? To copy plaster figurines and engravings, grind pigments, paint clothed portraits when necessary, to 'do' hands, drapery and hair. It was not much, but it was something. For many years Goya contented himself with borrowing from Lujan a palette which he, in turn, had adopted from Tiepolo.

Usually overloaded with work, Lujan occasionally advised his clients to commission one or other of his pupils to execute a mural or decoration. Although he was only seventeen, Goya had proved to be a diligent pupil who assimilated knowledge quickly and worked with unusual speed. Aided by the fact that he was

a 'local boy', he was entrusted with some paintings for
the parish church at Fuendetodos. Only someone very
wise or very foolish would have declined an opportunity
to shine in the village of his birth!

Both in Lujan's atelier and, a little later, in that of the
sculptor Juan Ramirez, Goya tried in vain to demonstrate
the lack of originality which was expected of him. A mad
whim prompted him to prefer the unknown capital to

THE EXPULSION OF THE JESUITS

Fuendetodos and Zaragoza, where he could have pursued a career on familiar ground in the shadow of the celebrated painters who lived there, such as Lujan himself or the elder of the Bayeu brothers.

When he finally departed with a few coins and his little notebook in his pocket, his painterly equipment, which consisted of guaranteed but hackneyed recipes, was meagre indeed; his cultural equipment was virtually non-existent. Father Joaquin of the Order of Scolopes had tried to instil the rudiments of an education into the three young *batturos*, Camillo, Tomás and Francisco, at the Escuela Pia which he directed at Zaragoza, but the teachers' level of knowledge barely exceeded that of their pupils. Francisco knew how to read and write when he decided to try his wings, but that was all.

This basic knowledge was not to be depised in a country whose inhabitants were largely illiterate. Besides, it was to the Scolope Fathers that Francisco owed something more precious than any cultural or material assets, the friendship of his fellow-pupil Martin Zapater.

Early endeavours

In Madrid in early spring of 1766, Francisco Goya started work on a painting entitled: 'Martha, Empress of Constantinople, presents herself before King Alfonso the Wise at Burgos and asks him for one-third of the sum stipulated as the ransom of her husband, Emperor Baldwin, by the Sultan of Egypt. The Spanish monarch ordains that she be given the entire sum.' Goya, now twenty, was confident that his picture would be enthusiastically received at the competition held during the summer by the Royal Academy of San Fernando, and that this would enable him to travel, all expenses paid, to Italy. Some ten other young painters, all fired by the same ambition, also laboured at the theme set by the board of examiners.

The jury met on 22 July 1766 to set the competitors yet another subject. This one, which had to be 'dashed

MAJA WITH A SHAWL, 1778. Etching after Velazquez

off' in two hours, was: 'In Italy, within sight of the
Spanish army, Juan de Urbino and Diego de Parades
discuss which of them shall be awarded the armour of
the Marquis of Pescara.' After this final test, the prizes
were to be distributed.

The presence on the Academy's jury of Goya's master,
Francisco Bayeu, who not only came from Zaragoza but

MAJA WITH A MANTILLA, 1778. Etching after Velazquez

was in favour at Court, did not prevent Goya from being as brusquely rejected as he had been when he entered the same competition two years earlier. The Academy's gold medal for 1766 went to Bayeu's younger brother Ramón, twenty years old like Goya himself.

At a period when the only two painters who enjoyed any authority in Spain – one the most brilliant representative of the older generation and the other the most active of the younger, Tiepolo and Mengs – were both foreigners, it was unlikely that any member of the San Fernando jury, even a native of Zaragoza like Bayeu, would have contemplated favouring the efforts of a surly and uncultured young Aragonese peasant like Goya – so typically, uncouthly and shockingly Spanish. He received no mention at all.

There is an Aragonese proverb which, like the story of Robert the Bruce, recommends one to try, try and try again, even when the situation seems hopeless. Francisco Goya had tasted defeat, but he was still at the beginning of his career. He did his best to succeed, listening to Bayeu's advice as he had to that of Lujan and Ramirez, imitating his masters assiduously and skilfully. But he made little impression. His clumsy manners, brusque way of speaking, rudimentary spelling – in short, his lack of education – put him at a disadvantage *vis-à-vis* pupils who were undoubtedly slower and less gifted than he was but more adroit in their social relationships and more generally 'presentable'.

Goya was still convinced that a gold medal would win him the respect of the unknowns with whom he rubbed shoulders every day in the streets of Madrid or those in antechambers of government offices, and he was not entirely mistaken in this assumption. His contemporaries reserved their esteem for painters who either had their origins in Italy or had spent a long time there. By awarding bursaries the Academy competitions, which Goya had twice failed to win, rendered possible both

foreign travel and the artistic initiation which it represented.

One of Goya's best biographers, Antonina Vallentin,
notes pertinently that 'Goya must have taken great pains
to succeed. He even seems to have rejected his natural
gifts in order to adapt himself to the cold and measured
style and simplification of pictorial values which constituted the official academic style which Mengs transmitted
to Bayeu and which the latter endeavoured to transmit
to his pupil. This rejection was so complete that it
extinguished all his natural tendencies towards vigour
and richness of colour.' Antonina Vallentin is alluding
in particular to the period when Goya, despairing of
being sent to Italy by an official jury, decided to get
there under his own steam.

Despite the legends surrounding the subject – Goya's
scaling of the dome of St Peter's, his abduction of a nun,
his meeting with David etc., none of which appears in
the least degree likely – it seems that the young artist
lived on a shoe-string during his comparatively brief
visit. With the little money he had managed to obtain
from his parents or scrape together by doing various
odd jobs – portering, copying, doing chores for more
fortunate friends, working for a troop of bullfighters –
Goya collected enough for his fare and embarked.

His arrival in the Eternal City went unnoticed. No one
paid any attention to the Spanish rustic who drifted,
sketch-book in hand, through galleries and studios.
When his savings had been dissipated he again resorted
to odd jobs. This state of affairs continued until he

INQUISITION SCENE

visited Parma, still in quest of the gold medal which he had failed to obtain in Madrid and now hoped to bring home from Italy.

Laurent Pécheux, the court painter, was a Frenchman from Lyons. He was also, and above all, a pupil of Mengs, just as Bayeu had been. Being a pupil of Bayeu, Goya did not hesitate to mention this qualification when he entered the Parma Academy's competition for the year 1771. The subject was: 'The conqueror Hannibal casts his first glance at the Italian countryside from the summit of the Alps.'

From Goya's point of view, the outcome was little better than that of the first two competitions at Madrid. The painter Borroni easily carried off the first prize. Whether or not he owed it to his status as a pupil of Bayeu, Goya this time won an expression of polite interest from the jury: 'The Academy notes with pleasure the good brushwork, the warmth of expression in Hannibal's gaze and the quality of grandeur in the general's pose.' It also noted, more severely, that 'Signor Goya's colouring is a trifle garish... He has handled the subject coolly... If his composition had deviated less from the subject set, and if he had put more realism into his colouring, he would have swayed the votes cast for the first prize.'

To someone who lived at a time when men matured early, a semi-defeat at the age of twenty-five – an age when fame should already be assured – must have seemed the gravest of setbacks. Francisco Goya returned home.

An Aragonese story tells how a *batturo* riding his donkey down a railway line chuckles as he hears a train whistling behind him: 'Whistle away! Why should I budge for you?' Goya reacted similarly to the misfortune that dogged him, but obstinacy in the *batturo* is not without an element of malice.   In Madrid, where everyone knew what went on in Rome, he would have been the man who had come back from Italy empty-handed.   In Zaragoza, where people were less *au courant,* his fellow-provincials greeted him simply as the man who had come back from Italy.

Eugenio d'Ors describes Goya as 'too much ruled by instinct to be calculating, too robust to be pushful'. If he is right, this may partly account for the lack of early success and explain why the unoriginality for which Goya strove with all due compliance and cunning bore such scant fruit.   He decided to embark upon his professional career with or without a medal.

The first tangible result of Goya's new policy came on 21 October 1771, when the Chapter of the Church of Our Lady of Pilar met to commission some frescos for the small choir.   Possibly attracted by the modest fee proposed, fifteen thousand *reales,* the board decided on Goya, stipulating that the unknown artist should first demonstrate his competence as a mural painter and then submit a finished sketch for approval by the Academy of San Fernando.   If he passed both tests the contract would be finalized.

Striking while the iron was hot, Goya submitted a fresco to the Chapter three weeks later.   It was approved, and two months afterwards he produced his sketch.

Anton Raphaël Mengs. SELF-PORTRAIT IN A RED CLOAK, 1744

The Chapter's remaining doubts evaporated. After inspecting Goya's design, a highly conventional affair embodying a court of fleshy angels adoring a triangle inscribed in Hebrew characters with the secret name of the Almighty, the whole floating in a sea of plump clouds, the canons sanctioned it without further hesitation. They even waived the right to consult the Academy, and Goya started on his fresco at once.

Six months later, on a fine July evening in 1772, wine flowed freely in the Goya home, where Francisco's entire family were celebrating his success in company with Zapater, his friend, and Lujan, his first master. The canons and dignitaries who had been invited to inspect the unveiled frescos were unanimous in extolling the artist's unusual speed and skill. Furthermore, since little was known at Zaragoza of the controversy between the post-Baroquism of Tiepolo's pupils and the neo-Classicism of Mengs, their praise came from the heart, devoid of partisan or ulterior motives.

Goya had, in fact, taken great care to preserve a discreet neutrality which would not shock one party or the other. A few traces of realism were detectable, notably in the bodies and faces of certain angels, but these were temperamental quirks of a minor nature and no one seemed to notice them.

Working rapidly and complying with his clients' tastes at fees lower than those charged by his colleagues, Goya enjoyed a growing reputation throughout the Zaragoza area, and commissions flowed in. At the Cartuja Aula Dei, the Carthusian convent near the town, he executed eleven enormous mural compositions in the decorative, stiff and dignified neo-Classical style. For the church at Remolinos, by contrast, he painted an ultra-pure Baroque treatment of Pope St Gregory, full of shapes which swirled in the contrasting light and shade. In the Sobradiel Palace at Zaragoza, for which 'something in the Italian manner' was requested, he calmly selected some Italian engravings and copied them on a larger scale with minor rearrangements.

Originality was a luxury. Only a painter who had 'arrived', who had already achieved fame and fortune, could afford to indulge in an occasional flight of fancy for his own amusement. Francisco Goya's ambition was not to build up an original *œuvre* but to become a painter of repute and, consequently, affluence. No one ever questioned the quality of his work. He painted quickly but meticulously, and the time was not far distant – as he must himself have realized – when his reputation would spread beyound the confines of his province and attract the notice of some aristocratic frequenter of the Spanish Court. After all, what was a great painter if not a painter of the great?

PORTRAIT OF CHARLES III IN HUNTING DRESS, 1780

'Bourgeoisification'

In the old days, a young man who wished to become a notary but lacked the wherewithal to finance his studies used to pass his legal examination and become clerk to a notary – preferably an elderly man approaching retirement, with a marriageable daughter and no sons anxious to succeed him.   The clerk married the daughter, received his training as part of her dowry, and duly became sooner or later a notary in his father-in-law's place.

This practice, which is still current today in certain professions, cannot be explained solely in terms of self-interest.   On the one hand, passions – even amorous ones – sometimes coincide with the wish to perpetuate them by cultivating them in a social context favourable to their growth.   On the other hand, someone who spends his time in a certain milieu is more likely to meet there, rather than anywhere else, the person with whom it seems logical to share the rest of his life.

LANDSCAPE WITH A LARGE ROCK, *c.* 1770

It was not until the nineteenth century that men emerged who, like Van Gogh or Gauguin, renounced everything in order to devote themselves heart and soul to painting. In the eighteenth century painting was still only an occupation or profession like that of the notary, lawyer, tradesman or industrialist. Velazquez, for example, married the daughter of his master Pacheco. Goya had scarcely heard of Velazquez at this stage, but he knew from his observation of fellow-artists that one ingredient of success was membership of a family of painters. His professional background would have to merge with his family background if he was to profit normally by the contacts and privileges which guaranteed the prosperity of an atelier.

Compared with Velazquez, who was already 'established' as a painter when he married at the age of twenty, Goya was ten years in arrears. It was not until he was approaching thirty that he carried out his first serious commissions and took advantage of his return to Zaragoza to court Josefa Bayeu, sister and ward of Francisco Bayeu.

They were married in 1775. It is clear that Josefa never doubted that Goya had married her because she was a Bayeu, and that Bayeu never imagined that Goya would have married her had she not been his sister.

'I need but little furniture for my house, for I think that, what with a print of Our Lady of Pilar, a table, five

LANDSCAPE WITH A WATERFALL, *c.* 1770

chairs, a stove, a cask, a guitar, a spit and a lamp, all else would be superfluous.'

Goya had been living in Madrid with Josefa for four years when he prepared to pay another visit to Zaragoza in 1780 and entrusted Zapater with the task of finding him lodgings as modest as his permanent quarters in Madrid.

He had made arrangements to leave for Madrid as soon as the marriage took place. No rumours of fame or reputation preceded him, but he knew that from now on he could rely on a staunch and powerful ally in the person of his brother-in-law. And Francisco Bayeu knew where his duty lay. What he might not have done to oblige a former pupil he now did in order to ensure that his sister's husband brought no discredit upon the name of Bayeu.

Within the context of his general plan to reform the fine arts in Spain, Anton Raphaël Mengs was taking an interest in the Santa Barbara tapestry factory, founded by Philip V on the lines of the Gobelins in Paris. Convinced that Santa Barbara could and should provide his Spanish pupils with a medium of artistic expression and a source of profit, Mengs decided to secure them commissions for cartoons on the subject of 'Spanish Life', i.e., genre scenes inspired by Flemish art. These were merely tapestries destined for the temporary adornment of corridors and drawing-rooms, not pictures intended to testify to the grandeur of human art and thought in the museums of the future. Since the medium of expression was 'vulgar', or popular, there was no reason why the subjects should not be so too.

Bayeu, who was the first to be consulted, produced some exemplary designs of his own and then put forward two names: those of his brother Ramón and his brother-in-law Goya. For Ramón, thirty years old and an Academy gold-medallist since 1766, this presented no problems. In the case of Goya, of like age but lacking any qualification save his relationship to the Bayeus, Mengs evinced far less enthusiasm.

In June 1776 an urgent order was received for some tapestries for the Prado residence of the Prince of the Asturias. Pressed by Bayeu and swayed by the fact that his other protégés, Ramón Bayeu and José del Castillo, were already engaged on cartoons, portraits or frescos, Mengs yielded. The factory would 'try out' Francisco Goya on condition that he accepted a provisional fee of 8,000 *reales*. It entered into no undertaking except in respect of the work in hand and offered him no sort of contract, as it did to other artists, tacitly or explicitly guaranteeing them a minimum number of cartoons per annum. Only too happy to be entrusted with an official commission for the first time, Goya apparently took no exception to such a proviso and set to work.

The Picnic on the Banks of the Manzanares ('La Merienda'), *The Doctor, The Parasol* and, some years later, *The Meadow of San Isidro* are among Goya's most typical essays in the art of tapestry. The first, sylvan and decorative, and the second, a narrative piece in the 'social realist' genre, responded to two of the dominant tastes of the century.

THE FLIGHT INTO EGYPT, *c.* 1770

SAN FRANCISCO DE PAULA, *c.* 1770

The third, despite its slightly derivative quality, heralds a Goya whom we have not yet encountered. As for *The Meadow of San Isidro,* it betrays Venetian influence, but the inverted triangle of the composition, the indestructible harmony that links figures, objects and countryside and, finally, the light which bathes the ensemble by virtue of the celebrated 'Goya grey', already in evidence here, encourage us to regard this as something much more than a cartoon.

Generally speaking, although the tapestries Goya undertook from 1776 onwards ('La Merienda' dates from 1782) show that he tried to please his public by mingling, at first with varying success but always with patience, intelligence and skill, styles borrowed from Italian, French, Flemish and even Spanish sources (e.g. Murillo), it should be noted that his 'cartoons' were conceived as genuine paintings – in other words, as finished works of art in themselves. At all events, his zeal was immediately rewarded: his cartoons found favour. Within three years he had produced thirty such pieces – ten more than Bayeu.

It would be wrong to dismiss Goya's tapestry cartoons as mere trifles. They were immeasurably better, more supple in execution, more realistic in colouring and considerably more imaginative than those of his competitors, notably Francisco Bayeu. They would not have been enough to win him the veneration of posterity, it is true, but they represent a significant stage in his artistic development. Even when he was past forty and enjoying the fame he had once seemed so unlikely to achieve, he continued to work on the themes of his former cartoons, purging them of all mannerisms alien to his own unique style.

Meanwhile, in 1777, Josefa had produced a son, Vincente Anastasio. A second son was born early in the summer of 1780, shortly before their return to Zaragoza. Goya wrote to Zapater announcing that he was a very handsome boy, a *muy guapo muchacho*.

Velazquez and the Academy

On 14 May 1824 Eugène Delacroix noted in his journal:
'Men of genius are made not by new ideas, but by an idea
which possesses them, namely, that what has been said
has not yet been sufficiently said.' At the beginning of the
last quarter of the eighteenth century, the promoter of
new ideas in Spain was Mengs.

Goya did not aspire to be an imitator or a perpetuator.
In any case, the little he knew of his predecessors' painting
did not encourage him to believe that 'what had been
said had not yet been sufficiently said'. Too intelligent
to be satisfied with copyist's work, too uncultivated and,
in this respect, uninspired to function as an inventive
imitator, he came into his own primarily as an 'arranger',
a role in which he excelled to a degree which could not
fail to gain him entry to the Academy sooner or later.

The year 1778 could have proved fatal to his career
as an official painter, which had just made such a promis-

ing, if belated, beginning. Unknown to anyone, himself included, 1778 did in fact mark the birth in Goya of a second personality, the one which astounded the world in later years and almost entirely obscured his earlier work.

Prompted by one of those miraculous whims which sometimes inspire even the most obtuse monarchs to take measures of general expediency in fields that are most alien to their personal temperament, and encouraged by a practice current among other European princes, Charles III suddenly remembered that the royal palaces contained innumerable paintings and decided that it would be good policy to show off what his forebears had acquired at such expense. He resolved to grant a number of painters access to his galleries and get them to make copies of the royal collection. This was how Goya, having been commissioned to make a score of engravings after Velazquez, first came face to face with masterpieces by one of the greatest painters who had ever existed and one who, like himself, was a Spaniard.

It was a tumultuous encounter. Hitherto Goya had made a habit of taking works for which he had no real regard and 'arranging' them in his own way. Confronted by Velazquez, he was dazzled – not only by the painter's extraordinary dexterity, his skill at preparing grounds, handling highlights or conveying a head of hair with a single brush-stroke, but by something which no sleight of hand, no 'trade secret' could explain: the mysterious presence of light which, on a plane surface occupied by specific shapes, could reveal a world of infinite and variable dimensions. Goya's practised eye soon discerned the manual tricks and trade secrets, but the rest – the true ingredients of Velazquez's greatness and genius, the majesty with which he celebrated the eternal drama written in the light and shade of every face, every section of wall, every tree and rock – filled him with such admiration that he forgot about his own talent.

Goya was aware that Velazquez had raised and solved some major problems. When he came to *Las Meninas,* that extraordinary picture which no one can look at without finding himself implanted amid the scene which it depicts – beside the painter, in front of him, behind him – Goya did not 'copy'; he sought to understand. What he tried to do was to strip away the 'flesh' of colour and reconstitute the black-and-white skeleton of the light in which *Las Meninas* is bathed, using bold hatched strokes to bring out the planes and counter-planes which give the picture its depth and animation.

No one can devote himself to this form of undertaking without feeling compelled to make a reappraisal of himself. Antonina Vallentin remarks that 'oddly enough, Goya is more in evidence in these reproductions than in his own works of the same period'. She continues: 'The memory of Velazquez's paintings remained with him always. Throughout his life he never hesitated to borrow poses, gestures, even landscape backgrounds from the master. Yet it was when he borrowed most flagrantly that he was at his most individual.'

Apart from having discovered engraving, which he henceforth practised on his own behalf, was he destined

PORTRAIT OF JOSEFA BAYEU (?), *c.* 1798

SELF-PORTRAIT (?), 1775

to plough the same furrow as Velazquez, a painter regarded as 'outmoded' by the contemporaries of Mengs and Bayeu? This would have meant forsaking the career of official painter which he had been diligently striving to pursue for years. Fortunately, he was weaned from the temptation of becoming an 'archaistic' painter by an event of unusual importance. 'Never, believe me', he wrote to Zapater, 'could I have wished for more as regards my work.'

Thanks to recommendations from an unknown source, Goya one day mounted the ornate staircases of the Royal

Palace and bowed enthusiastically to a short, elderly gentleman with a face like a weasel's. Beside him stood his son, the Prince of the Asturias, a fat youth with a beatific smile. Maria Luisa of Parma, his young wife and future queen, watched the painter with a cold black eye as he unpacked his paintings for inspection. Her thin lips pursed themselves into an expression of condescending interest. A stroke of good fortune like this had to be exploited. Farewell Velazquez! The triumphal road to the Academy now lay open to an artist who, if only during the brief ritual of hand-kissing, had been favoured with the sovereign's gaze. Mengs died in Rome on 29 June 1779 and was laid to rest at Raphael's feet in a magnificent tomb in the Pantheon. Goya, declaring himself to be 'a pupil of the Royal Academy of San Fernando', requested the honour of being admitted as a member of that institution. He was unanimously accepted on 5 July 1780.

Bayeu, who had just been appointed Rector of the Academy and had succeeded Mengs as senior Court painter, continued to play the role of paterfamilias with undiminished perseverance. Not content with stage-managing his young brother-in-law's electoral campaign, he went to the lengths of furnishing him with a study for his test piece, a Christ on the Cross. Having copied the study and carefully removed anything that might have offended lovers of depersonalized dignity, Goya produced the coldest and most meaningless picture imaginable, adopting the requisite neo-Classical style. Not even Bayeu could have achieved such perfection.

A title is not an automatic passport to fame, as Goya, too easily intoxicated by his electoral success, soon discovered. An artist's honour is a delicate matter and one on which his reputation and means of livelihood depend, for as soon as his reputation becomes dimmed by a small shadow his prosperity disappears altogether.'

Although an Academician, Goya was nonetheless compelled to ask his friend Zapater to help him draft a petition to the Chapter of Our Lady of Pilar. Having devoted part of this to an explanation of the economic and moral importance of a painter's reputation, he went on to claim the right to execute on his own a commission which he had originally accepted in the capacity of a subcontractor.

In 1774, three years after Goya's 'cut-price' decoration of the small choir of Our Lady of Pilar, Francisco Bayeu had painted a Coronation of the Virgin beneath the cupola. Since his contract covered other frescos which he had no time to carry out, Bayeu had persuaded the Chapter to allow Goya and his own brother Ramón to complete the work under his direction and in his name.

The head of the Bayeu family was naturally indignant when Goya, who owed him everything from bread and butter orders for tapestry cartoons to his recent admittance to the Academy, decided to break the contract and claimed the right to 'perform alone the part assigned to him... and this in the presence of several persons of this city'. Amazed by the sudden discovery that his dutiful pupil could be 'arrogant, proud and intractable', Bayeu decided that, if he was so keen to act on his own responsibility, that was precisely what he should do.

ÆSOPVS

Sacada y grivada del Quadro original, de D. Diego Velazquez, que existe en el R.ᶫ Palacio de Madrid, por D. Fran.ᶜᵒ Goya Pintor, año de 1778. Representa a Esopo el Fabulador de la estatura natural.

AESOP, 1778. Etching after Velazquez

THE PARASOL, 1777

Bayeu did Goya a disservice by washing his hands of the matter in this way. In vain did Goya complete – within ninety days – a fresco which was no more and no less original than any to which either of his brothers-in-law could have lent their name. Bereft of Bayeu's support, he amounted to nothing. Criticism poured in from every quarter. His figures were adjudged indecent, his composition poor, his colouring ill-chosen. To crown his humiliation, the Chapter forbade him to paint any of the quoins until he had secured the approval of Bayeu, with whom, as everyone knew, he was at loggerheads.

Goya's lengthy petition to the canons served no purpose. In vain did he complain bitterly of his brother-in-law and 'the hypocritical way in which he let it be known that his unwillingness to accept responsibility stemmed from generosity'– which amounted, in Goya's estimation, to 'arousing the Chapter's misgivings'; in vain did he denounce the envy which had, according to him, prompted Bayeu to discredit him. In the end he was forced to make honourable amends and effect a reconciliation with his brother-in-law, which meant submitting once more to his tutelage. Not to have done so would have been tantamount to declaring war in a lost cause, for Goya could count on no one's support– not even that of Josefa.

Reason dictated surrender, but such was the shame and fury in his heart that he could not refrain from airing his grievances to the parochial board when he went to collect his fee. His fellow-townsmen reacted to the insult by insulting him in turn: the board made a habit of distributing gold medals to artists who had helped to decorate the church. One of these was bestowed on Josefa Bayeu because, it was emphasized, her status as Bayeu's sister entitled her to it.

In a country which shared in what the historian Arnold Toynbee was to call 'the civilizations of honour', Goya's humiliation and disappointment threatened to have grave repercussions on his life and work.

Discouraged, he returned to Madrid, where he nursed his grievances and neglected his art. His response to Zapater, who urged him to paint, was: 'As to the picture, I shall do it. It is enough that you ask me to, but only your friendship could make me do so, believe me. When I think of those times in Zaragoza, my painting burns me alive.'

'These princes are angels!'

The success for which he had yearned so long came
to Goya when he approaching forty, at the very moment
when, 'burned alive' by his painting, he was thinking
of giving everything up.

Shortly after his disconsolate return from Zaragoza,
the architect Ventura Rodriguez recommended that he
should participate in the decoration of the Church of San
Francisco el Grande. Rodriguez had designed this building in a cold and stately style which accorded with the
canons of neo-Classicism. Vast sums had been lavished
on its construction over a period of years, and all Madrid
was impatiently awaiting the day when the faithful could
attend the first service in what public rumour already
held to be a sort of Christian Parthenon. The Court
had taken a special interest in the venture, which meant
that it was vitally important for any painter to be one

of those privileged to adorn it with their work. What was more, this was the first time Goya had secured an important and, from the point of view of his career, vital commission without owing it to the good offices of Francisco Bayeu.

'I was much cast down, but it has pleased God to comfort me', he wrote to Zapater, who now received a string of triumphant communiqués, almost all of which were accompanied by tactical advice. Goya was determined to make the most of this opportunity to 'confound the vile slanderers' who had shown such scant faith in his ability. He even requested the royal secretariat to send a letter to the dignitaries of Zaragoza, informing them in the most unequivocal terms that the painter whom they had scorned was now participating, by royal command, in a work of national importance.

Goya's letters to Zapater contain little reference to the fact that he had only been engaged to decorate one of San Francisco's seven subsidiary altars, or that the decoration of the main altar had been entrusted to Francisco Bayeu. The accent is laid, needless to say, on his own share: 'His Majesty having decided to commission paintings for the Church of San Francisco el Grande, the Court has done me the honour of designating me to be entrusted with an order.' Better still: 'My friend, the time has come for the greatest venture in the realm of painting that Madrid has ever witnessed.'

At the end of three years, during which he sadly neglected his work for the Santa Barbara factory, Goya scored a brazen triumph. Although his painting, *San*

THE DOCTOR, July 1779 - January 1780

Bernardino of Sienna preaching before René d'Anjou, King of Sicily, was scarcely distinguishable from those of his colleagues except that he depicted himself in the patron saint's congregation, it was greeted as favourably as those of Francisco Bayeu, Maëlla, Ferro or Castillo – and perhaps even more so – both by the personages invited to the consecration of the church on 8 December 1784 and by the throng of curious spectators.

Contrary to what one might suppose, his first personal successes coincided with abrupt moods of tension. Every-

49

thing that happened suggests that he was simultaneously satisfied and infuriated with himself. The death of his father and his sister Rita undoubtedly affected him, but not to an extent which would explain his repeated spells of depression, of artistic impotence and irritation with his contemporaries, whom he suspected of banding together to persecute him.

In fact, Goya's San Francisco 'triumph' proved to be more a victory for his prestige than his pocket. He, Ferro and Castillo, not yet celebrated enough to dare ask for payment in advance, only received their fees after bombarding the authorities with petitions. Their account was eventually passed for payment by José Moñino, the small time 'lawyer' who had been created Count of Floridablanca by Charles III, whose Prime Minister he was. He scribbled in the margin: 'Although the pictures are not worth much, the ones by these three are the least bad.'

Floridablanca had commissioned Goya to do a portrait of him. Why? The only known portraits by this unknown artist were a bad one of Don Pedro de Alcantara de Zuñiga, fourteenth Count of Miranda, executed in a pedestrian style in 1777, and another of Cornelius van der Goten, director of Santa Barbara – a fine example of the portraits which Goya was to produce in such numbers but one whose realism was then thought to be in bad taste. If Goya was anxious to paint the Prime Minister in 1783 it could only have been in order to impress potential clients.

He was not paid in cash, however. José Moñino, Count of Floridablanca, rewarded him in other coin.

Not only did he deign to help Goya thread his way through the tangled undergrowth of officialdom, but, had it not been for this unpaid portrait, Ventura Rodriguez would never have dared to recommend him to the Infante Don Luis, younger son of Ferdinand VI and Elisabeth Farnese, who wanted a painter sent to Arenas de San Pedro, his estate in Castile.

Don Luis was as surprised at the speed with which Goya could produce an elegant portrait in a single morning as he was to learn that a painter, by definition a man of humble birth, could derive as much pleasure from the chase as he did himself. Hunting gaily on a great estate in the company of its owner, a prince of the blood, the little Aragonese poacher comported himself so well that Don Luis never tired of telling everyone: 'Upon my word, this dauber *(pintamonas)* is as mad about hunting as I am!'

When a member of the royal family said that of someone, his fortune and that of his family was made. Goya's brother Camillo was given the chaplaincy of Chinchon, a reputable and remunerative appointment which he celebrated by commissioning Goya to produce an *Ascension of the Virgin*. In 1783, Goya embodied a likeness of himself in the group portrait of the Infante's family – his first essay in this genre. (He had done so in every one of the pictures that had marked an important stage in his career to date: timidly in Our Lady of Pilar, then in San Francisco el Grande and again, quite recently, in the portrait of Floridablanca.) Despite a certain stiffness and crudity in the distribution of light round the

CRUCIFIXION, July 1780

THE PRISONER, 1778

central figure, the picture may be compared with his celebrated *Charles IV and His Family*, painted seventeen years later but already foreshadowed in this piece. He had now reached the vitally important stage when he had ceased to be merely a reputable painter, and was becoming a fashionable portrait painter.

Two years later, in 1785, the Infante Don Luis died, but by then Goya's career was too well-established to be menaced by the removal of his patron. Other doors opened to him, notably that of the Duchess of Osuna, under whose protection he was destined to work for almost a quarter of a century. As he entered the gates of the Alameda, the Duchess's palace, Don Francisco de Goya murmured the words which he had uttered on leaving Arenas: 'These princes are angels!'

The end of a career

On 21 September 1789, which marked the end of mourning for the death of Charles III, there was dancing in the streets of Madrid. There was also dancing in the stately homes of the great. Framed in an illuminated oval, portraits of Charles IV and Maria Luisa adorned the façade of the Osuna mansion. They were the work of Goya, who had not painted so many royal countenances since executing a lifelike portrait from memory of the deceased king in hunting costume four years earlier. Governor Campomanes and the Ministro de la Gobernación had both consulted him on the decoration of their residences.

A change was about to take place in the life of Spain, just as a change had already occurred in Goya's. As early as August 1786, he had written to Zapater: 'I am so overwhelmed with work that at this moment I do not know

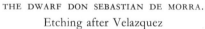

THE DWARF DON SEBASTIAN DE MORRA.
Etching after Velazquez

PRINCE BALTHASAR CARLOS, 1778.
Etching after Velazquez

which way to turn nor, more especially, how to fulfil all the obligations I have accepted.'

In the years since he had painted Floridablanca's portrait in 1783, Goya's order-book had gradually turned into a sort of Who's Who. He had frequently made deletions in or added to the little genealogical guide which his mother had drafted for him twenty-five years before, when he was setting out for Madrid as a still beardless youth. However, the framework of these noble families had scarcely changed, except that sons had some-times replaced their fathers. Goya put a cross in front of each name whose owner had paid to sit for him. There were more and more of them as time went by.

SELF-PORTRAIT, 1783

General Ricardos, the Count of Gansa, Ministro de la Hacienda, the young Don Manuel Osorio de Zuñiga, various members of the Osuna family and relatives of the Infante Don Luis were among the first to be painted in this period – which takes us up to 1792 – and Sebastian Martinez, art collector and Treasurer to the General Council of Finances, was among the last.

Prices varied according to the importance of a portrait and the quality of the sitter. In the case of the Osunas, for instance, Goya asked a thousand *reales* for each preparatory sketch and twelve thousand *reales* for the completed picture. This meant that a single picture could earn him twelve to fifteen thousand *reales,* equivalent to the annual income with which he had, a short time ago, declared himself 'the happiest and most contented man in the world.'

Other portraits were done for the sake of love or friendship. His sitters included Josefa and Francisco Bayeu, both portrayed with great expertise, his friend Zapater and the historian Ceán Bermúdez. The portrait of Bermúdez was a rather scamped affair because he had only earned the honour by procuring an influential client in the person of François Cabarrús, a Bayonne merchant. Cabarrús had moved first to Zaragoza and then to Madrid, where he set up a soap business before founding the Bank of San Carlo, of which Bermúdez was an employee. The various directors of this bank came to Goya in turn, and the information which the artist gleaned in the course of these sittings enabled him to invest his savings profitably. These must have been substantial, for he did not

confine himself to the Bank of San Carlo but wrote to Zapater in May 1789 asking where he could profitably invest a hundred thousand *reales* which he did not know how to dispose of.

Goya had already produced his 'Four Seasons' tapestry for the bed-chamber of the Infante Gabriel, future husband of Doña Ana Victoria de Braganza, and was soon to be entrusted with a portrait of Charles IV, destined for Capodimonte, seat of the Neapolitan royal family.

In the Goya home, birth followed birth at intervals of nine months or so – an unbroken succession of still-born or sickly children which was interrupted in 1784 by the birth of Javier, the only son to survive. However, Goya's domestic misfortunes alone were not enough to account for his renewed fits of depression, less frequent than in earlier years but no less acute. His *Self-portrait with Candles* (on his hat, to enable him to paint at night), produced towards the end of 1786 or in early 1787, shows him looking thin and irritable. He was not wearing well, and he bitterly resented the increasing burdens of age. In a letter to Zapater he wrote: 'I have grown old, with so many wrinkles on my face that you would never recognize me if it weren't for my flat nose and sunken eyes... I am feeling my forty years with a vengeance...'

In the social sphere, all that remained for Goya was to become painter to the Albas as well as the Osunas; but this was a delicate matter. Being mistresses of the two greatest houses in Spain, the duchesses were ipso facto rivals. Each had her own dressmakers, painters, bullfighters and actors, and it was impossible, on the face of things, to serve Alba and Osuna at the same time.

Malicious gossip alleged that Goya could not produce a good female portrait unless he had – in biblical language – 'known' his model. This was to credit him with impro-bable powers, since his good female portraits were considerably more numerous than his good male portraits – and these were already innumerable!

THE GREASY POLE, *c.* 1787

Every difficult moment in Goya's career saw the emergence of a woman whose portrait he had painted and who intervened – with almost invariable efficacy – on his behalf. But this does not mean that she was necessarily one of those he had possessed in his studio, modestly veiling his statue of the Virgin of Pilar in advance. It may be added that none of his mistresses, with the exception of the last, ever complained. of his rebuffs, churlishness or terrible fits of jealousy. Even though she had been Goya's mistress, the Duchess of Osuna did not take exception when his services were solicited by the Duchess of Alba, despite the predictable consequences of such a move.

Why were the many women in his life so forbearing with him? Looking closely at his portraits of society women, one can see that they were painted without indulgence but with unmistakable love and a generous sensuality which manifested itself in the harmony between his choice of colours and the personality of his model. How could women resist such a magician or bear him a grudge when he left them with a vision of themselves which was richer and more positive than they could ever have imagined?

Goya could be ruthless with male sitters, but the psychological tension of his female portraits is pre-dominantly benevolent. The detestation apparent in *The Old Women* may have stemmed from his personal fear of approaching old age – but that is another story.

In the sphere of official recognition, Goya still lacked titles which would have distinguished him from his fellow-Academicians. It was with an eye to this vexed question that he had triumphantly written to Zapater in July 1786: 'Martin, I am Painter to the King, with fifteen thousand *reales!*' In fact, through the good offices of Maëlla and Francisco Bayeu, he had merely been awarded a fixed salary by the Royal Tapestry Factory, for which he had already been working for more than ten years.

A year earlier he had taken his appointment as *pintor del rey* in place of Calleja for granted, but he had to be content with the title of sub-director of the painting class at the Academy of San Fernando, beating his long-time rival, Gregorio Ferro, by nine votes to four.

Still in the sphere of official recognition, June 1788 marked yet another setback. Feeling strong enough to challenge Bayeu once more, Goya opposed him in the election for the Directorship of the Academy. The result: Francisco Bayeu, ten votes; Maëlla, six; Goya, nil. It was the accession of Charles IV, an amateur painter like his wife Maria Luisa, which broke Goya's run of bad luck. In April 1789, even before the coronation festivities had taken place, the King deigned 'to appoint Don Francisco de Goya y Lucientes *pinter de camara,* with all the privileges which this office enjoys today'.

The waiting was over. Goya was now entitled to a salary and the title of 'Excellency'. All that remained, after taking his ailing wife for a change of air in Valencia, was to return to Zaragoza in October 1791 and savour his triumph. Local bigwigs who had virtually hounded him from the city ten years earlier competed eagerly for

THE MEADOW OF SAN ISIDRO, 1788

the honour of being painted by him. Among the portraits produced during this stay were a new one of Zapater and the chilling portrayal of Canon Don Ramón Pignatelli, to whom Spain owed the completion of the Aragón Canal and its first 'labour exchange', the Casa de la Misericordia.

Nevertheless, in the interval between his appointment and his visit to Zaragoza, Goya had been subjected to one final humiliation. Passing through Madrid on his return from Valencia, he learned that Ramón Bayeu had not only received an order for tapestry cartoons from the Santa Barbara factory but had been given an increase in salary. Preening himself on his new title, the *pintor de camara* thereupon took umbrage and refused to go on working for the factory. It is impossible to tell how things might have turned out if family feeling had not impelled Francisco Bayeu to intervene yet again.

Goya went back to work with ill grace, churned out some cartoons modelled on his previous work, and admitted to Zapater that his behaviour towards Bayeu during the previous ten years might possibly have been ill-advised: 'I greatly regret that relations between us have been strained, and constantly pray God to rid me of the spirit of pride which always overwhelms me on such occasions. If I manage to observe moderation and do not fly into any more rages, my actions will be less evil for the rest of my days.'

But the course of his life was already determined. On his return from Zaragoza he was struck down by a terrible illness. No one expected him to survive, and he was so dazed and paralysed that it seemed almost preferable that he should not. 'The nature of the illness is so terrible that the thought of his recovery fills me with melancholy', wrote Francisco Bayeu, and in one sense he was right. The Goya who was his undisciplined pupil but his pupil for all that, the Goya who would, if his *œuvre* had ended there, have been thought of a good painter 'in tune' with his times and the author of a number of portraits, some landscapes and a few frescos revealing traces of a trend which others were to develop, the Goya who was an official Spanish painter of the eighteenth century, 'died' in 1792. He was forty-six years old.

'Fantasy and invention'

Christian theologians teach us that the most perverse
of men – indeed, even the most mediocre – may at any
moment be touched by divine grace. Comparatively
speaking, the accident which occasioned Goya's artistic
'conversion' could not have been very different in essence
from the one which resulted in St Paul's spiritual conversion on the road to Damascus.

If one carefully analyses the following passage from
a letter written to Bernardo Yriarte, the Duchess of
Osuna's accredited poet, on 4 January 1794, it is clear
that the man who competed with Bayeu for the honour
of painting some insipid and conventional murals and the
man speaking here are two different people: 'In order
to occupy an imagination mortified by the contemplation
of my misfortunes, and to recover part of the great
expenditure which they have occasioned me, I have

THE SWING, 1787

THE STILT-WALKERS, *c.* 1788

started work on a group of cabinet paintings in which I have managed to make room for the observation which is customarily absent from commissioned works, which do not allow one to exploit one's fantasy and invention.'

These triumphs of fantasy and invention depicted scenes inspired by popular Spanish festivals and ceremonies: *Carnival Scene* ('El Entierro de la Sardina') and *Procession of Flagellants* in 1793, *The Bullfight* and *The Madhouse* in 1794. They are by the hand that was to paint the dome of San Antonio de la Florida and the nightmarish murals in the Quinta del Sordo. All Goya's genius is already there. No one ever managed to convey the various aspects of the human comedy, whether tragic or comic, with such charm and fluency. It would be malicious to say that such a painter owed everything, or almost everything, to Bayeu and Mengs. His strong and masterly distribution of light and shade is reminiscent of Rembrandt and his fluent brushwork of Velazquez – but a wilder and more elemental Velazquez.

The Academy of San Fernando, for whom the pictures in question were destined, expressed its collective pleasure at seeing them – a polite and mollifying formula designed not to disturb the invalid's convalescence. Hypothetical paroxysms of genius on the part of this desperate, violent and often aggressive man inspired less awe than his fits of 'insanity'.

The inaccuracy and confusion prevalent in documentary records of this period, particularly medical records, make it impossible to determine the exact nature of Goya's strange malady. He seems to have been afflicted by a paralysis which completely robbed him of sight, speech and hearing for several weeks. This stunned condition was succeeded by several months of appalling and unbroken delirium, both auditory and visual. His head rang with strident and unendurable cacophonies, and he was drawn down into a world teeming with monsters which prowled round him and assailed him from every side. But little by little his strength returned. He survived the ordeal and his hallucinations turned first into

nightmares and then into drawings, etchings and paintings. Yet the price of victory was high: at the age
of forty-six Goya was stone-deaf. He remained so until
the end of his long life.

This peculiar case has aroused the interest of many
modern doctors. One of these, Dr Le Guen, having
rejected some of the more fantastic theories and made
an honest reappraisal of the subject, confines himself
to the following conclusion: 'All that is certain is that
a diagnosis of general paralysis or even cerebral syphilis
cannot be upheld, principally because Goya did not die
until thirty-five years later, a month after suffering
a stroke at the age of eighty-two, without ever having
exhibited the slightest symptom of mental deterioration.'

What is equally certain is that after this attack, which
his robust constitution enabled him to withstand, Goya
re-emerged as the Goya we know today. The cautious
petit bourgeois of yesterday was soon to become notorious
as the lover of the turbulent Duchess of Alba, and when
he picked up his brush, pencil and burin again he startled
himself before proceeding to startle the world.

He was fascinated. Thanks to his illness, a window
had suddenly and miraculously opened upon an unknown
land peopled with living lights and shadows and terrifying
beings, a land which one glimpse had imprinted upon
his mind for ever. Was it a dream? The time was not far
hence when Spain, ravaged by the Napoleonic wars,
would dream a dream no less terrifying and unforgettable.

Too many people have tried to attribute Goya's genius
to his alleged insanity. Of Dr Henry Ey's assertion that

FESTIVAL AT THE HERMITAGE OF SAN ISIDRO, 1789

'the essence of madness is to *be* an aesthetic focus rather than to *perform* an aesthetic function', Dr Le Guen rightly remarks: 'There are painters who rave and madmen who paint, there are those who paint madness and those who rave pictorially, but there is no "insane painting", just as there are no psychopathic works of art.'

THE ATTACK ON THE COACH, 1787

Goya's visions, as far as we can judge from his graphic records of them, never for a moment suppressed or distorted reality, but analysed it with a keenness which verged on cruelty. Omnipresent to the point of obsession, the tangible world was constantly evoked in such a way as to live again with ever-increasing intensity under his abstracted and magical touch. In essence, Goya's art was based upon observation and did not seek to devise arbitrary or imaginary forms and shapes. Some contemporary critics have thought that certain blemishes in his *lavis* and his swarms of obsessional monsters foreshadowed a surrealistic form of painting or even a painting entirely devoid of any ties with reality. On all the available evidence, however, it would be mistaken to claim Goya as the ancestor of the painters who seek their inspiration in the automatism of would-be spontaneous movements. 'I had three masters', he said in later life, 'Nature, Velazquez and Rembrandt.' It is significant that Nature came first.

Anatole France makes Napoleon assert that he invented nothing in the realm of strategy. 'He thought no further than the humblest grenadier in his army, but he thought with unprecedented force and vigour.' Goya did not invent anything either. He had seen everything he painted or drew, but he saw it – monsters and all – with unprecedented sensibility, intelligence and intensity. His deafness, which remained with him throughout his thirty-five remaining years of life, left him no alternative. His only means of communication with the world were two eyes and a hand which expressed what those eyes saw.

Maria Teresa, Duchess of Alba

Francisco Bayeu, who died in August 1795, made his last intervention in Goya's life and career in the spring of 1794. In his capacity as head of the family, he was obliged to furnish a certificate to the effect that his brother-in-law was in no fit state to work on the tapestry cartoons which he had promised to Santa Barbara. Since the factory manager, Livinio Stuiks, had been compelled to announce the sick man's breach of contract ('he is entirely prevented from painting in consequence of a grave mishap that has befallen him'), Bayeu felt it his duty not only to vouch for the facts but to quash prevailing rumours of Goya's 'fall from grace', which threatened to drive his clients away.

Bayeu couched his affidavit in cautious terms. Convinced that the recent pictures in which Josefa's husband had given free rein to 'fantasy and invention' betokened

SPRING, June 1786

an enfeebled intellect rather than burgeoning genius, he wrote: 'Although it is true that Don Francisco de Goya has undergone a grave illness, it is equally true that he is a little better, and that he is painting, though not with the enthusiasm and perseverance of yore.'

Nevertheless, it was this period which gave birth – apart from the 'cabinet pictures' already mentioned – to the second and admirable portrait of La Tirana, a Tirana already touched by the corrosion of old age, and to that of Colon de Larreategui. Both of them, the first more unabashedly 'Goyesque' and the second more conventional, are illuminated by a strange light whose presence can be detected in only one of Goya's earlier portraits (that of van der Goten).

This light, though due largely to the juxtaposition of well-chosen colours and the masterly subtlety of the half-tones which lend vibrancy to the space between his planes, also stems from a certain state of mind which recurs throughout his subsequent work, whether euphoric or otherwise. This applies to all his paintings, engravings and drawings – from the implacable *Charles IV and His Family* to the agreeable *Milkmaid of Bordeaux,* from the astringent *Caprices* and the horrors of the *Disasters of War* to the triumphant sensuality of *The Maja Nude* and the dozens of children's heads which Goya always painted with such passionate tenderness, as though to exorcise his gnawing personal obsession with old age.

The first portraits of the Duke and Duchess of Alba also date from the period when, according to Bayeu, Goya was not painting 'with the enthusiasm and per-

THE WINE HARVEST, autumn 1786

WINTER SCENE, 1786

severance of yore'. Did Goya know the Duchess of
Alba before 1795, the year which marked the real beginning
of the association which was destined to have such
a profound effect on his life and work? Some people
believe that they can identify the features of Doña Maria
del Pilar Teresa Cayetana, thirteenth Duchess of Alba,
in the eighteenth-century-style compositions which Goya
produced some ten years earlier *(The Swing, Blind Man's*

Buff, etc.). Others envisage Maria Teresa tenderly nursing the invalid and gradually succumbing to a feeling of love compounded as much of pity as of admiration – not that this romantic hypothesis is out of keeping with her imaginative and generous nature.

It is not implausible to suggest that Goya may sometimes have been inspired by the face and form of the beautiful and all-powerful duchess, whom he had doubtless seen in the course of some official or social function. On the other hand, it seems unlikely that he would have risked his still vulnerable career by openly frequenting the home of the main rival of the Duchess of Osuna, his patroness, and of Queen Maria Luisa, to whose patronage he aspired. Only the impunity which a sick man sometimes enjoys could have prompted him to behave so audaciously.

Maria Teresa, in whose memory the Duchesses of Alba still bear the name which she herself never used (Cayetana), was thirteen when she married the nineteen-year-old bridegroom who had been selected for her, Don José Alvarez de Toledo Osorio Perez de Guzman el Bueno, eleventh Marquis of Villafranca, a chronic invalid whose only passion in life was music. He died in 1796, twenty years after his marriage and a year after Goya painted him beside his harpsichord, a melancholy figure with a sheaf of Haydn songs under his arm.

The marriage contract stipulated that the Duchess should retain the majority of her possessions 'in complete independence of her husband... whatever her place of residence'. The Marquis additionally undertook to bear the title of Duke of Alba. What was at stake, apart from the survival of a name, was the perpetuation of a family fortune which put the Albas on an equal footing with numerous European kings, including the Bourbons of Spain.

Maria Teresa's grandfather, a noted Spanish ambassador to the court of France, went about escorted by a jester who wore his innumerable decorations and orders for him. He was a grand seigneur who alternated between moods of rage and refined urbanity, between pride in the peerless splendour of his name and terror at the thought that his name might die with him. He had only one son, a cultured nobleman of liberal disposition who knew and corresponded faithfully with Rousseau. When the son died prematurely, Maria Teresa, his granddaughter and sole descendant, was eight years old. In the absence of a male heir, it was incumbent on her to provide the missing link in an illustrious chain. Her grandfather would have been plunged in despair had he known that she would never become a mother, but this did not prevent the Alba name and, to a lesser extent, the Alba fortune from surviving until our own day.

The little girl grew up not only in the shadow of this tall figure hewn of medieval granite, but also in close contact with her mother, Doña Mariana de Silva y Sarmiento, Duchess of Huescar, a figure who symbolized the broadminded liberality, charm and thirst for knowledge of the eighteenth century. An amateur poet and painter, Doña Mariana was fond of gilded Bohemianism, unfaithful lovers and French Encyclopaedists.

THE DEVIL'S LAMP, 1789

Neither her first widowhood nor her second, nor even her third marriage, succeeded in subduing the vigour of her romantic sentimentality. On the death of Mariquita Ladvenant, a fashionable actress of the period, Doña Mariana promptly adopted one of her four children, a putative son of the Marquis of Mora, who had consoled her for the loss of her first husband without forgoing the favours of the beautiful actress. When the Marquis died, Doña Mariana remained faithful to her faithless lover's memory by marrying his father, the Count of Fuentes, an elderly hidalgo who had been ruined by his Parisian debaucheries. When the latter died in his turn, the Duke of Arcos succeeded him.

No amount of misfortune ever affected Doña Mariana's gentle and devoted nature. She reigned over arts and letters, patronized those who pursued them, translated French plays for the Madrid stage and presided, in her capacity as Honorary Director, over the destinies of the Academy of San Fernando.

Two such conflicting influences might well have unbalanced a young person less fitted for independence than that of Maria Teresa, the future Duchess of Alba. She confined herself to inheriting from her grandfather his sense of absolute superiority to the common herd and from her mother a scorn for convention.

When she met Goya or, rather, when she effectively entered his life, she was thirty-three and he forty-nine. A self-portrait painted at about this period shows us the restless eye and drawn features of a man who is recuperating from a grave illness. As for her, her emotional excesses and turbulent life do not appear to have affected her youthful character and physical appearance. Quite the contrary. She skipped along like a young girl, but with the grace and assurance of a mature and lovely woman. We are told that she occasionally borrowed a dress from one of her lady's maids and slipped off to take part in public festivals. On one such occasion a young seminarist followed her into a tavern. The unfortunate man not only had to satisfy the whim of his new conquest by giving her his last sou and leaving his breeches behind as security, but was obliged to wrap his coat round his bare legs and escort the pseudo-maidservant back to the Alba mansion, where she claimed to be employed. Invited to return next day, the poor young seminarist was received by her in the great hall, surrounded by a brilliant gathering of friends whom the Duchess had carefully informed of her practical joke in advance.

Although she matched bullfighters with the Duchess of Osuna and gowns with the Queen, she begrudged neither the intellectual authority of the former nor the political power of the latter. To her, life was a theatre in which to perform – always to the limits of scandal or absurdity – a never-endingly successful play starring Maria Teresa, Duchess of Alba. She dreamed, and her dreams stirred, shocked, dismayed and confounded the adult world. They were the dreams of a cruel, sentimental, grandiloquent and laughable woman, but dreams which, thanks to her immense wealth, no material obstacle had ever prevented from becoming reality.

Why should she have picked on a painter when she was so little interested in art and artists – and why this ageing, deaf and disagreeable commoner, when she loved

SUMMER, 1786

dancers who impressed her with their elegance and bull-fighters with their virility? One could answer this question by posing others. Why, for instance, should the way-ward duchess have lovingly reared a little Negro girl named Maria de la Luz? Why should she have supported, amongst other human derelicts, a lame and stammering old monk called Brother Basil? '*Amigita de mi alma* (little friend of my soul)', she remarked to a woman friend who had come upon her naked one day in her summer residence, 'if it embarrasses you, I'll cover myself with my hair.'

This was the woman who ordered copies of the Queen's latest gown from Paris and dressed her maidservants in them. This was the woman of whom Godoy, when he had risen to power via the boudoir of Queen Maria Luisa, wrote in later years: 'The Duchesses of Al – and Os – competed for possession of Costillares and Romero, the leading matadors of the period. No one talked of anything but this ignoble excess. People discussed the episodes, the outbursts of passion, the generosity of the two rivals, but no one was shocked by their immorality.' This was the woman who stroked Goya's troubled brow and murmured words of comfort and love which he could not hear.

In August 1795 Francisco Bayeu died, and on 4 October of the same year Goya was elected to succeed his brother-in-law as Director of the Academy by ten votes, as against eight cast in favour of Gregorio Ferro. His salary was fifty doubloons. While awaiting 'an attenuation of his ills' he did not, however, immediately take up the post which prior to his illness would have represented the summit of his ambitions. Two years later, in April 1797, he renounced it for good because he felt 'on the verge of seeing his afflictions increase rather than diminish'. The Academy appointed him an honorary director and took the opportunity to express its profound regret at seeing 'a teacher of such eminent merit in such a deplorable state of health, one of his ailments being a deafness so acute that he hears absolutely nothing, not even the loudest noises'. It is amusing to note how Goya – destined as he was to become an octogenarian –

always referred to his poor state of health when it enabled him to evade official duties without renouncing any of the attendant benefits.

In June 1796, while Goya was allegedly anticipating 'an increase in his afflictions', the Duke of Alba died at Seville. Four months later Goya installed himself at Sanlucar on the banks of the Guadalquivir, where, remote from Madrid and the court, the Duchess was spending her period of mourning.

PORTRAIT OF DOÑA MARIA IGNACIA ALVAREZ DE TOLEDO,
MARQUESA DE ASTORGA, CONDESSA DE ALTAMIRA, AND HER DAUGHTER,
c. 1789-1790

PORTRAIT OF THE CONDESSA DEL CARPIO, *c.* 1792

Drawing, the universal language

It was not the first time that Goya had haunted one of those paradisial domains where the great of the world were said to live a life sheltered from care and uncertainty. We have already seen him dazzled by the few weeks he spent on the estate of the Infante Don Luis and over-joyed by his sojourn with the wealthy and intelligent Duchess of Osuna.

The Osunas and Don Luis only received him as a producer of portraits and decorative paintings. At San-lucar, where fortified Moorish villages and trees trans-planted from African oases were mirrored in the vast and voluptuous expanse of the Guadalquivir some leagues distant from Cadiz and Seville, Goya was no longer a humble purveyor to princes but the favourite of a queen who was unencumbered by the weight of a crown and unconstrained by royal etiquette. He could imagine himself a sort of prince consort – a prince in his own right, if only for the duration of a widow's mourning.

All the evidence suggests that he had access to the widow's bed, but that he was not, in all probability, the sole recipient of that privilege. He was not scandalized by this. It would have required all the bourgeois hypocrisy of the nineteenth century and all the democratic prudery of the twentieth to make him attach undue importance to the fact that, as one whose birth and destiny had placed him on the fringes of high society, he was flouting the rules of common morality.

There is no written record of Goya's stay at Sanlucar. So effective was the conspiracy of silence designed to observe the conventions where the young widow was concerned and to spare Josefa's feelings that it even eliminated the existence of credible oral traditions. The only evidence we possess is unwritten and unspoken but highly explicit in its eloquence. It is signed 'Goya'. Piously iconoclastic hands have torn out the more intimate pages, but some of the drawings from the notebook in which Goya recorded what he saw are still extant.

In his introduction to the two-volume edition of Goya's drawing from the Prado, Sánchez Cantón rightly remarks that 'in company with Alonso Cano and, if we descend the scale, Francisco Pacheco, Antonio del Castillo and Francisco Bayeu, he is one of the very few Spanish painters who, unlike Greco, Ribera, Zurbarán, Velazquez and even Murillo, left drawings behind.'

'Goya', he added, when publishing *Cent dessins de Goya* in conjunction with Félix Boix in 1928, 'is a draughtsman

THE MANNIKIN, 1791-1792

PORTRAIT OF DOÑA TADEA ARIAS DE ENRIQUEZ, *c.* 1792-1794

in his drawings, not a painter who uses pencil, pen or brush to solve the problems of his paintings in advance on a sheet of paper.' One has only to leaf through the few surviving sketches made at Sanlucar to realize that they were neither preliminary sketches for paintings nor studies designed to 'keep his hand in'.

Drawing was drawing to Goya, but it was something else as well. Not only did he absorb a scene in all its vividness and describe it, but his description was accompanied by a value-judgment. To go on from there to speak of Goya's 'expressionism' would be only a short step, but one which it would be imprudent to take.

Picture a deaf man who was considerably older than most of the men and women who composed the gay society around him. Picture him drawn into a vortex of merry-making, intrigue and idle tittle-tattle which he observed, not like a silent film in which words are mimed, but like a 'talkie' with the sound-track removed. In his desire to understand, participate and follow the story, he had to visualize the completion of curtailed gestures, scan faces for the meaning of the words he could not hear, dramatize the interplay of moving shapes. He sought less to record the expression of others than to converse with them by expressing himself, that is to say, by using his pencil to say what he thought of them.

We are left in no doubt as to his lively sense of appreciation when he drew the outlines of the Duchess's body as she held the little Negress Maria de la Luz to her breast. Nothing could express urgency of desire more poignantly than the drawing of his patroness pulling up her stocking. And, when he depicts a soldier turning his back on a girl who casts him an oblique look of wistful disappointment, it is easy to imagine what they would have said to Goya and what his reply would have been.

Goya's graphic style goes far beyond caricature or even simple expressionist 'reportage'. Properly speaking, his drawing, like the etchings which amplify it, is a form of meaningful handwriting placed at the service of what he was to call the *'idioma universal'* or universal language. Goya's drawings are ideograms more than anything else. There used to be a long-standing belief that he distorted them at the dictates of mood or whim. Not at all. They are the nouns, verbs and adjectives of his personal idiom. He puts them in the plural or singular, in the present, past or future, in the feminine, masculine or neuter. Nothing could be more intelligible, and the sole reason why this language took so long to decipher was that people did not realize it was a language at all.

The language of the Sanlucar drawings recurs throughout his subsequent work, as does his language of fear (monsters, the giant in the clouds), of joy (children, beautiful girls radiant with health), and of revulsion (elderly procuresses, bloodthirsty soldiers, corrupt priests). Goya's personal bitterness and artistic authority had both increased in the interval between his first portrait of the Duchess pointing to his name, humbly traced in the sand in place of a signature, and his 1797 portrait of her, which bears the name 'Alba' on the setting of the

CARNIVAL SCENE ('EL ENTIERRO DE LA SARDINA'), 1793

PROCESSION OF FLAGELLANTS, 1793

ring on her third finger and his own name on the ring adorning her extended index finger.

On his return from Sanlucar, where he had produced drawings but very few paintings, he paid a visit to Zaragoza. His old friend Zapater scarcely recognized him. They had little in common now, the wealthy provincial merchant who had consoled Goya during his years of obscurity but was now merely a reminder of them, and the deaf painter who had suddenly become a protégé of duchesses. They continued to correspond, ever more rarely and in ever more formal terms, for another three or four years, but their long friendship was drawing to a close. 'Flattered by fortune, the painter was destined to breathe an air which was far from pure, and one which was bound to intoxicate him', Zapater's heirs commented sadly when they published Goya's letters in later years.

Times had indeed changed, and not only for Goya. While the balmy night air in Sanlucar was throbbing to the gentle strains of the guitar, mobs were growling the Carmagnole in Paris, and while Godoy was plotting the downfall of the Count of Aranda on Queen Maria Luisa's pillow, having previously accomplished that of his predecessor Floridablanca, a Bourbon's head rolled, and the Marseillaise, chanted lustily by the executioners of Louis XVI, embarked on the conquest of Europe.

There was a feeling that something ought to be done. Popular opinion was unanimous that the Bourbons owed it to themselves to assist their French cousins, if only symbolically. Godoy, already Prime Minister, garbed himself in the uniform of Captain-General of the Armies. The smugglers of the Sierra Nevada sent an *élite* body of well-equipped men and Spanish forces occupied the French province of Roussillon, but there was a manifest disinclination to take sterner measures.

'No one approved of the violent course of the French Revolution,' Godoy wrote in his memoirs, 'but people willingly embraced the theories that had engendered it; an armed crusade was viewed with reluctance.' Godoy exchanged his Captain-General's uniform for the even more gorgeous attire of 'Prince of the Peace'. To avoid alienating France, Spain began by ceding part of Santo Domingo in 1795. A year later she unreservedly placed her fleet at the disposal of the Republic, thereby taking sides against England in a war which was destined to drag on for twelve years. It resulted in the total anni-

PICADOR ATTACKING A BULL

hilation of the Spanish navy, her last remaining instrument of power, and the blockade of Cadiz, her sole means of communication with her possessions in the New World.

Constricted on land by the obligations of an alliance with France and on the sea by a youthful English fleet which was to defeat the old and invincible Armada, Spain became little more than an island doomed to gradual suffocation. Domestic peace still reigned, at least outwardly. The people were docile, the aristocracy complacent. There was dancing in the village squares, whispering and intrigue in the corridors of the royal palace.

Was it his deafness that enabled Goya to see further and more clearly than the others? No strains of gay

THE VILLAGE BULLFIGHT, 1794

music ever reached his ears, nor did the sound of elegant
chatter which masked events whose importance no one
could gauge, but anguish seized him at the sight of this
ballet danced by mute and carefree figures on the soil
of a country – his country – threatened with extinction.
Beneath the smiles of the Duchess's Sanlucar intimates
he could already detect the grimaces of horror which
impending disaster was to imprint upon those same
untroubled faces. Goya's idyllic pastoral and boudoir
scenes recur in a modified form in the tragic, harsh,
despairing world of the *Caprices,* which he now started
to engrave.

THE MADHOUSE, 1794

The Caprices

'In Spain, engraving begins with Goya's *Caprices*,' asserts Jean Adhémar in *La Gravure au XVIIIe siècle*. Although the process had been known for a long time, it was hardly ever used except as a means of reproducing and disseminating works of art (as, for instance, when Goya was commissioned to engrave a number of pictures from the royal galleries, among them several by Velazquez, at the behest of Charles III). Engraving – at least in Spain – had not hitherto emerged as an autonomous branch of the graphic arts. With the ninety-two plates comprising *The Caprices,* on which he worked between 1794 and 1799, Goya not only reached one of the most significant stages in his own development but ushered in a whole new era in engraving itself.

Piranesi and Rembrandt, whose engravings figured on the walls of Goya's house from now on, had each displayed incomparable mastery, one by glorifying the metaphysical aspect of architecture and the other by conveying the radiance of a new form of harmony. In England, the engraver's technique had been used by Hogarth to raise satire to the status of art and by William Blake to carry fantasy to the threshold of genius. There had been realistic engraving, satirical engraving and poetic engraving. But there had never before been an engraver who, like Shakespeare in his plays, combined realism, satire and poetry at one stroke. That engraver, undoubtedly the greatest of all time, was Goya.

André Malraux tells us that Goya 'discovered his genius the day he ventured to *stop pleasing.*' The theory is an attractive one, but is it tenable? Yes and no. Yes, in that the illness which afflicted Goya abruptly released him from his obsessive desire to please at any price, and did so at the very moment when he had at last begun to achieve the success he craved. No, because Goya never wished nor dared to displease by deliberate design. He remained subject to the same sporadic depressions and changes of mood throughout his new life. He was still sly and vindictive, endowed with genius but uneasy. His deafness compelled him to use first drawing and then etching and painting as a language which completely satisfied his need for intellectual intercourse, not simply as a means of expressing particular reactions to the world of shape and colour which it is the painter's function to explore. One has to absorb the syntax of a language and learn its vocabulary before one can accept it as such. In the meantime, its unintelligible assonances tend to sound absurd.

The assertion that Goya ventured to 'stop pleasing' is only a half-truth. *He could not afford to stop pleasing* because his infirmity had suddenly transported him into a world where the problem of communication was inseparable from that of survival.

Like the *Disasters of War* and *Proverbs* of later years, the *Caprices* represent a sort of diary in which Goya jotted down impressions and his interpretations of them, i.e., in which he recorded the world of reality as it appeared to him after it had passed through the sieve of his personal judgment.

Sometimes, when he takes the stage himself, the *Caprices* become a sort of romantic confession, but even his confessions are integrated into the structural context of a moral observer's notebook. What is more, he discarded a large number of plates in order to assure his works a continuity and homogeneity which would make them 'readable' – not that the latter term necessarily implied 'easy reading'.

'Although he refrained from "ridiculing anyone's individual failings",' says André Malraux, 'his art was so disconcerting and the public so inclined to pass judgment on an artist rather than follow him, that for fifty years the *Caprices* were regarded as pictorial fables interspersed with fantasies...'

PORTRAIT OF THE DUCHESS OF ALBA, 1797

SELF-PORTRAIT (AGED FORTY-ONE), 1787

Minds such as André Malraux's, which are well-equipped to analyse and understand the phenomenon of artistic creation, are still interpreting Goya's three hundred or so etchings one by one, each in its imaginary context. No one thinks of them any longer in terms of 'stylistic exercises', still less as the fruits of a secondary occupation subordinate to that of painter. What is involved is a veritable *'recherche du temps perdu'*, an investigation of a given temperament and period, scene by scene and group by group. The personal phantoms which haunted Goya more than once when he was at death's door are as much in question as his subtle recollections of the joys and sorrows of Sanlucar, of idle strolls through the streets of Madrid, of musings amid the rugged sierras of his childhood, of the horrors of the Inquisition and the no less horrifying miseries of daily life, of the gorgeously clad monstrosities in whose antechambers the painter had lingered for so long, hoping that they would deign to sit for him.

Disregarding a few preliminary ventures, the *Caprices* marked the start of Goya's career as an engraver of aquatints and etchings. (Lithography, which he was one of the first artists to use, was still to come.) It is possible that the idea for them came to him while he was convalescing at the Cadiz home of his friend Martinez, a collector of engravings and the possible source of his Piranesi and Rembrandt prints.

English engravings had been finding their way into Spain for some time past, and the country was witnessing a growing trade in prints, both anti-revolutionary cartoons and pieces of republican propaganda secretly imported from France. Resemblances between the latter and certain of the *Caprices* are certainly not coincidental. For example, one celebrated French cartoon depicted, first, a wretched peasant bent double beneath the weight of a nobleman and a priest, and, second, the same peasant forcing the two men who had ridden him to carry him in triumph. A scene from the *Caprices* shows two men bent double under the weight of two donkeys. The inscription: 'They cannot help it.' A complementary engraving depicts two old men perched on their lackeys' backs, playing at bullfighting like children. The inscription reads: 'Now one, now another.' The commentary on the same engraving: 'Such is the way of the world: people mock and make sport of each other; he who yesterday was the bull today plays the caballero, the picador. Fate presides over the festivities and allots roles according to her whim.'

Finally, the milieu in which Goya developed – a milieu which comprised both the aristocracy and 'intelligentsia' of Madrid – was deeply impregnated with the new ideas. As in all the turbulent periods which have foreshadowed crucial and violent phases in the history of mankind, many writers and artists tended to translate into their own idiom the repugnance they felt for an established but tottering order from which they wanted to dissociate themselves at all costs.

Lacking the power to form a political party, a number of kindred spirits founded a society called the Acalophiles (lovers of ugliness), one of the main instigators being

PORTRAIT OF FRANCISCO BAYEU, 1795

the poet Moratin, with whom Goya took refuge at Bordeaux many years later. To evince a passionate interest in ugliness in a country which claimed to represent harmonious traditionalism, as contrasted with the ephemeral chaos of revolutionary republicanism, was to imply that ugliness existed in Spain and that, consequently, Spain could not be the best of all worlds. To make ugliness conspicuous and systematically attract public attention to it was, in a sense, tantamount to advocating the overthrow of the established order. From time immemorial, authoritarian regimes have rightly regarded as a direct attack on themselves any attempt to portray, graphically or in writting, characters which do not accord with the sense of docile contentment which they have decided to impose on their subjects.

There is no doubt that the influence of the Acalophiles endowed the *Caprices* with a highly individual and 'modernistic' flavour. If they lacked detailed written commentaries it was, first, because Goya's genius did not lend itself to verbal expression and, second, because the Acalophiles were closely watched by the Inquisition and the royal police. If one of them remarked that it would be a fine day tomorrow, he risked being thrown into gaol for months on suspicion of having proclaimed the forthcoming liberalization of the regime. If, on the other hand, he wrote phrases of like calibre at the foot of a Goya print, the speaker would be Goya, a celebrated figure who enjoyed the protection of the Albas and of the royal family, a man whom the Inquisition might seek to intimidate but would hesitate to persecute.

'There are antecedents and coincidences,' Jean Adhémar says of the *Caprices,* 'but there is, above all, the master's genius, without which all this life and movement would have remained in darkness...' It is disconcerting to leaf through this admirable series, print by print. 'The cards are shuffled,' was the verdict of Lafuente, who believed that Goya deliberately intended to shock his audience by the 'brutal nature of the transitions'. It might equally be conjectured that he acted from a prudent desire to disguise the existence of 'explosive' cycles.

In fact, the group deals with three or four subjects. The first is woman: the contempt her love deserves and the contempt she feels for man. There is nothing to choose between men and women *(Birds of a Feather Flock Together)* and their love is as worthy of scorn as that of the dogs depicted in the foreground of another of Goya's etchings. Secondly, Goya shows that it is impossible to communicate, that man is isolated in a tower or prison, that he is a stranger even to himself *(People Do Not Know Themselves).* Thirdly, there is social satire of an extremely virulent and topical nature directed against ignorance, charlatanism, self-conceit, voluntary or involuntary deafness, people who padlock their ears, ambition, clerics who exploit superstition (Eat That, You Dog!), popular suffering and misery in general, to which the only answer is sleep and silence. Finally, Goya transports us into the world of magic and sorcery. Anxious to present his dreams and visions with 'the solid testimony of truth', he simultaneously assures us that 'the dream of Reason produces monsters...'

PORTRAIT OF LA TIRANA
(THE ACTRESS MARIA DE LAS MERCEDES ROSARIO FERNANDEZ), *c.* 1793

Replying to the question 'What is a *Caprice?*', André Malraux says: 'An illustration to a caption? Most of the latter were added to the drawing, sometimes as interjections, even commentaries. "Bravissimo!" – "Who would believe it?" – "See how serious they are!" – "Bon voyage!"... He draws as if in a dream and, in *Visions of a Night,* was to draw his dreams themselves... This obsessed genius is obsessed with own creations, and his over-precise dreams resemble drawings more than his drawings resemble dreams.

'After engraving captions to his figures, he adds commentaries to them. Beneath the flying demons in *Bon Voyage* he notes: "Where is this hellish crew going, filling the air with its cries?" He categorizes them: "These", he remarks beneath the etching called *Little Devils,* "are of quite another kind: gay, amusing, obliging, perhaps a trifle greedy and prone to play pranks; nevertheless, good-natured little fellows." "If you had not come at all", he writes, less ironically, beneath another, "it would not have been unduly regrettable..."

'Certain phrases are more intriguing: "What a curious thing that these creatures only like to be seen at night and in the gloom. No one can tell where they shut themselves up and hide in the daytime. If anyone should be lucky enough to discover a goblins' lair, seize them and exhibit them in a cage it would be worth a fortune to him..." He never speaks of them as if he controlled them. By "fantasies" he means principally unforeseeable things. He receives such images rather than premeditates them. They are less dream-images than day-dreams... People had been pursuing them for centuries.'

The social criticism latent in the *Caprices* was quite as calculated to alert the Inquisition as was Goya's sudden proliferation of unruly monsters, which it was the Inquisition's duty to combat under the name of 'deviltries'.

In 1610, a coven of witches from Logrono which used to meet at the 'He-Goat's Meadow' (Aquellare) had been 'purified' in its entirety by the fires of the Inquisition. In 1798, Goya painted a scene showing the He-goat blessing some aged and repulsive witches (a theme which he revived on the walls of the Quinta del Sordo in 1820), as well as a series of other pictures of the same type, destined to adorn the reception rooms of the Duchess of Osuna. Diabolism was all the rage, and it was this particular aspect of Goya's genius which Baudelaire referred to in *Les Fleurs du Mal*:

> *Goya, cauchemar plein de choses inconnues*
> *De fœtus qu'on fait cuire au milieu des sabbats*
> *De vieilles au miroir et d'enfants toutes nues,*
> *Pour tenter les démons ajustant bien leurs bas.*

Publication of the *Caprices* was scheduled for 1797 but did not come into effect until 19 or 20 February 1799, and then for only eighty etchings out of ninety-eight. Even then, Goya took elaborate precautions, one of which was to precede publication by an announcement in the *Diario de Madrid* couched in the careful language of a business contract.

He defended his choice of subjects in advance: 'The author, persuaded that the criticism of human errors and vices (however seemingly dependent upon eloquence and poetry) may also be the object of painting, has selected from among the manifold extravagances which are common to all civil society and from the vulgar preoccupations and snares sanctioned by habit, ignorance or self-interest, those subjects for his work he has deemed capable of providing material for ridicule and, at the same time, of exercising inventive imagination.'

He also defended himself: 'Painting (like poetry) chooses from what is universal that which it estimates to be best suited to its ends: it unites, in a single fantastic personage, circumstances and characters which Nature represents as being distributed among several subjects; and from this ingeniously arranged combination there results a felicitous imitation, thanks to which the artist, by a skilful artifice, acquires the title of inventor and not that of servile copyist.'

His rhetorical precautions were in vain. Barely forty-eight hours after their publication, the *Caprices* were withdrawn from sale. Everything suggests that Goya and the Inquisition had engaged in a trial of strength, and that he may have withdrawn the *Caprices* rather than be compelled to do so by official decree, thereby embroiling himself in a scandal. The fact remains that, although he was indicted by the Holy Office, no one knew of this until he admitted it himself twenty-five years later.

How was the affair hushed up? Another man might have succumbed to the dangerous temptation to play

PORTRAIT OF A YOUNG WOMAN
(POSSIBLY THE DUCHESS OF ALBA), *c.* 1795

the martyr by defending his good faith before a tribunal which was determined to convict him, but this was not the type of adventure to appeal to Goya. While there is no doubt that his influential connections helped, the gesture which really saved him derived from his personal fund of instinctive caution and peasant cunning: 'Foreigners are most desirous of acquiring them (the *Caprices*), and lest they fall into their hands after my death, I wish to make a present of them to the King, my master, for his collection of engravings,' he wrote to Charles IV.

As though it would have been unseemly and pretentious to give the King a present unless he accompanied it with a petition, Goya humbly requested Charles IV for an allowance, not for himself but for his only surviving son Javier, who, he asserted, had a genuine talent for painting and should be enabled to travel abroad to exploit it.

Once the plates of the *Caprices* were safely installed in the Royal Collections, the Inquisition's activities ceased. Meanwhile, Godoy suffered a temporary fall from grace and Don Mariano Luis de Urquijo came to power. A scholarly nobleman who had consorted with the Encyclopaedists and was a translator of Voltaire, Urquijo dreamed of recalling the Jews to Spain, of abolishing slavery in America and even of putting a brake on the temporal powers of the Church. Goya's portrait of Urquijo is an unenthusiastic one, but it was from him that, barely seven months after the *Caprices* scandal had been averted, he received a letter which he had been eagerly awaiting ever since the death of Bayeu, who shared with Maëlla the post of First Painter to the King,

PORTRAIT OF GENERAL URRUTIA, 1798

and who had never been replaced. This letter, dated 31 October 1799, read:

'Wishing to reward your merit and, in your person, to give the arts a testimonial which may stimulate all the masters, and to prove to you the esteem in which he holds your talent in the noble profession you have embraced, His Majesty has graciously appointed you First Painter of the Chamber with an annual salary of fifty thousand *reales;* an additional five hundred ducats annually will be allotted to you for your carriage, and His Majesty further wishes that, in the event that he should pre-decease you, you should occupy the house now used by Don Mariano Maëlla.'

San Antonio de la Florida

Goya had come a long way since the days when a few thousand *reales* were enough to provide him with a sense of well-being and security. And his salary as First Painter to the King represented only a minor proportion of his income. Both at Court and in the city, everyone with any claims to opulence sat for him and had their apartments decorated by him. He very rarely left his own premises now. Instead, people danced attendance on him. An inventory of the apartments which he occupied during the closing years of the eighteenth century shows that, in an age in which furniture was scarce, his home boasted no less than forty-six chairs and ten or twelve stools upholstered in gold damask for the use of his visitors – clients, friends and hangers-on. The furniture in his waiting-room was quite as sumptuous as that in the country houses and mansions of the great.

THE WITCHES' SABBATH ('EL AQUELARRE'), 1798

One item which attracted particular attention was a magnificent cupboard painted blue and black. His library was valued at 1,500 *reales* and his coffers contained a collection of jewels – mainly diamonds – to the value of about 55,000 *reales.*

Goya was noted for being a shrewd businessman, but what aroused even greater interest was the choice of pictures on his walls. First, there were some favourite works of his own. These included a portrait of the Duchess of Alba wearing a black mantilla and, in the dining-room, a dozen still-lifes. The latter probably resembled the two now in the Prado and foreshadowed the still-life techniques of Chardin and Soutine just as *The Milkmaid of Bordeaux* was to embody the whole of Renoir. The pictures on his walls which did not bear his own signature provided an indication of where his fundamental tastes lay: a Correggio, two portraits by Velazquez (possibly Velazquez's portraits copied by Goya himself), ten Rembrandt etchings, four by Wouwermans and a series by Piranesi.

If the *Caprices* had not indicated the existence of dissatisfaction in his innermost heart, coupled with an anguish of mind which foreshadowed the *Disasters of War,* Goya's fame, wealth and influence between 1796 and 1802 might have stamped him as being at his artistic zenith. His ease of execution, felicitous colouring and infallible sense of composition all suggested that nothing would ever disturb his equilibrium again.

As usual, he continued to paint numerous portraits, and, as usual, there was a substantial amount of dross

THE CAPRICES: 'PRETTY TEACHER', 1799

among them. It was not that he devoted more time and care to the better ones. It was simply that some faces and forms inspired him while others did not. In the former case, the result was a well-balanced masterpiece executed in bold brush-strokes which could be clearly distinguished at close quarters but which melted away when viewed from a distance to be replaced by an impression of great homogeneity and exactitude.

Bursts of vivid colour are rare. In *Lady with a Fan* (1799), the 'values' of the hair, mantilla and even of the lightly sketched landscape background have been neutralized, as it were, to allow the light to play on the face which constitutes the essence of the picture and on the bent right arm which lends emphasis to the subject's pose.

In a portrait like that of Guillemardet, a member of the National Convention, close relative of Delacroix's father and French Republican Ambassador to Madrid (painted in 1798 and now in the Louvre), Goya deliberately allowed the light to play not only on the features of the sitter but on the tricolour sash at his waist and the tri-colour plume adorning the hat on the table beside him.

The admirable *Man in Grey* (a portrait of Goya's son Javier, born in 1784) dates from 1798, and the two *Majas,* clothed and nude, were also painted on the thresh-old of the new century, as was the remarkable *Charles IV and His Family*. Similarly, it was during this period that Goya painted the frescos in San Antonio de la Florida, the chapel where his bones have lain since they were brought back from Bordeaux.

On 1 August 1798 a carriage could be seen waiting outside Goya's Madrid home to take him to the banks of the Manzanares. Here stood a brand-new chapel, a miniature basilica which had been designed and built by the leading architect of the neo-Classical school, Juan de Villanueva. It was constructed in the form of a Greek cross surmounted by a central dome.

During the preceding two months and in the interval between making two studio studies of 'St Anthony bringing a dead man to life to make him confess the name of his murderer and exonerate one who is innocent', Goya had already paid repeated visits to the chapel in order to study the shape of the dome, measure the walls

THE CAPRICES: 'IT'S HOT', 1799

and calculate the angles of the four pendentives, seven tympanums and various arches.

For four months from 1 August onwards the carriage made the same trip every day, returning each evening with its passenger wrung with fatigue and creative fervour. San Antonio was to St Peter's what a hunting-lodge is to Versailles, but Goya realized that he was engaged on the decoration of his own Sistine Chapel. It was no longer a question of an altar or a few panels, as at Zaragoza or San Francisco el Grande. The whole interior of San Antonio would bear Goya's signature, just as the Sistine bore Michelangelo's.

Some art historians have declared themselves surprised that a work which they regard as joyous and serene should have been conceived by an artist who was simultaneously preoccupied with the hallucinatory visions of the *Caprices*. Possibly because they are difficult to see and can only be admired *in situ,* these frescos have not always attracted the attention they deserve.

We know that Goya painted them in an unusually hectic frame of mind. In fact, judging by the four months he spent on them, he must have painted and repainted them several times over. The few people who witnessed his labours recalled the scene with stupefaction and awe. A deaf and bulky figure ensconced on the scaffolding beneath the little dome, he moved about agitatedly like a bull in the arena, but an intelligent bull who was determined not to give ground until he had conquered both toreros and public. He flew into terrible tantrums when his washes ran down the wall. Ordinary brushwork became too slow for him, so he tied bunches of rag to the end of long poles, ordered sponges by the pound and furiously daubed in the areas to be occupied by faces and bodies, trees, mountains and sky.

Many people have interpreted it as a manifestation of an ancient pagan instinct – indeed, a deliberate desire to 'laicize' a Christian shrine – that Goya's fresco incorporated likenesses of useful friends and connections, from the Duchess of Alba and Godoy to the *majas* and *majos,* the urchins, peasants and beggars who made up the human spectrum which he encountered every day in the street or on country roads. This, however, is as fallacious as it would be to assert that the people of the Middle Ages lacked religious faith because they adorned their cathedrals with scenes from daily life. Despite the feverish way in which Goya tried to adapt the exacting spontaneity of his creative inspiration to the general requirements of composition, the dome of San Antonio gives the impression of a well-balanced masterpiece, both in the spiritual and technical sphere. What can be seen behind the balustrade which encircles the dome in accordance with a formula borrowed from Tiepolo's frescos for the Villa Contarini is, in fact, an extremely faithful projection of the drama of death and resurrection which is re-enacted *below* when priest and congregation celebrate Mass.

Let us put ourselves in the place of the priest. What does he see when he turns to bless the congregation and raises his eyes to heaven? A whole world of men and women, some attentive, others intent on their own

business and others dreaming, but each looking as if he or she had been placed there by the painter's brush in order to testify that the tragedy of the Redemption which is being enacted on the altar concerns the sum of humanity as it actually is.

Let us now put ourselves in the place of the congregation. Above the altar, St Anthony's miraculous restoration of life to a dead man in the interests of justice

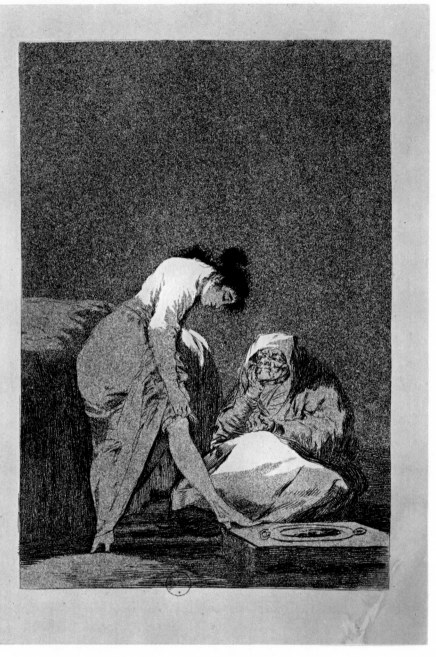

THE CAPRICES: 'THEY MUST FIT TIGHTLY', 1799

is an·extension of the liturgical theme. Another noteworthy feature – remarkable enough in a Spanish work of art and even more so in one by Goya – is that the object of St Anthony's miraculous attentions, although dead, looks less macabre than faintly optimistic.

The bold execution of the San Antonio frescos relates them to the Quinta del Sordo murals which Goya was to paint twenty years later in the bitter contemplation of his own solitude. Their general spirit and their profound urge to lend pictorial expression to the forms of public worship also relate them to a whole series of major paintings on the theme of the Mass. These include *The Grotesque Marriage* and *The Churching* (1815), and, more especially, *The Communion of San José de Calasanz* and *The Prayer in the Garden of Olives,* which are among the loftiest expressions of mysticism in Christendom.

Such is the evidence which enables one to state that Goya's indisputable anti-clericalism was far from being a symptom of atheism. Besides, was he not a compatriot of St John of the Cross, who died thanking God for not having ordáined that he should be a bishop? As for the angels who were, so to speak, 'slapped' on to the walls in an eruption of wholly sensual joy, some people regard them as archaistic throw-backs. Others – and their point of view does not necessarily conflict with the preceding one – believe that by endowing the angels with human form the artist was striving to convey that mankind has been redeemed not only in soul but in body.

Just as the engraver found inspiration and freedom of expression in the *Caprices,* so the painter found them

in these frescos, which possess all the charm of the eighteenth century, all the inventive fury of the nineteenth
and all the fervour which characterizes great painting of
every period. It is no mere coincidence that Goya's
mortal remains now lie at the foot of the main altar in
San Antonio de la Florida.

The space devoted here to the San Antonio frescos
and to subsequent paintings on the subject of the Roman
Catholic Mass in no way implies that Goya should be
regarded as an essentially mystical painter. It simply
means that, besides being an engraver, mural painter,
portraitist, landscapist and caricaturist, he was also a
religious painter – a fact which has not in general been
sufficiently stressed.

Was he motivated by a wish to 'look good' in a country
dominated by the Inquisition? This theory would not
be incompatible with the shrewd and realistic side of his
nature, but its likelihood fades when we are brought
face to face with paintings such as *The Churching, The
Prayer in the Garden of Olives* and *The Communion of San
José de Calasanz*. We then realize that they were handled
with the same freedom or, rather, with the same sense
of release, as 'imaginative' pictures such as *Carnival Scene*
('El Entierro de la Sardina'), *The Madhouse,* etc., painted
immediately after the illness which almost killed him
at the age of forty-six. On the threshold of old age,
Goya was increasingly haunted by memories of his
childhood, and continued to be until the end of his days.
In his tapestry cartoons, e.g. *The Greasy Pole,* he often
made a point of depicting children playing the country

THE CAPRICES: 'TILL DEATH', 1799

games which he and his brothers had played as youngsters.

The bogey-man had grown up, too, however. He had turned into a shrouded giant who, to the sadly imprudent adults of the *Disasters* and the *Caprices*, signified universal fear. (Cf. Goya's commentary beneath the plate entitled *Here Comes the Bogey-man* in the *Caprices*: 'Injurious misuse of early education. To bring a child to fear the bogey-man more than his own father, and so to make it afraid of what does not exist.' Spanking is not forgotten either. *The Pitcher Broke,* the twenty-fifth plate in the *Caprices,* depicts 'educational' corporal punishment with a cruelty which is combatted by the moral contained in the caption: 'The boy is a scamp and the mother bad-tempered. Which of the two is worse?'

The benches of the Escuela Pia in Zaragoza, where the Scolope Fathers had taught Goya the rudiments of writing, remained equally vivid in his mind. Mme Tallien, who loved Spain like many French people but found it a hard country to understand – i.e., found it impossible to conceive that a people so closely related to her own could not keep in step with France after seven centuries of Moslem occupation – delivered a harsh but, in a sense, just verdict on education in Spain towards the close of the eighteenth century: ' "The boy shows a proper humility," say the priests when they wish to praise one of them, meaning that he has already acquired a monkish subservience, self-abasement or, if you prefer, diffident hypocrisy.'

Be that as it may, the Scolope Fathers do not seem to have complained of a lack of humility in the pupil whom

P. 2

El si pronuncian y la mano alargan
Al primero que llega.

THE CAPRICES: 'THEY SAY "YES" BUT GIVE THEIR HAND TO THE FIRST MAN
WHO COMES ALONG', 1799

THE CAPRICES: 'POOR LITTLE THINGS!', 1799

posterity was to regard as the personification of artistic rebellion. Although Goya frequently pilloried the priest-policemen and corrupt monks who brought disgrace upon the Spanish clergy, he never turned against his first teachers. Indeed, it was for the Church of the Order of Scolopes that he painted his famous *Communion of San José de Calasanz,* half a century after receiving his meagre education under the auspices of that Order.

What was more, despite a business sense which verged on avarice, he declined payment.

Even when he blasphemed, even when throttled by the garotte of the Inquisition, a Spaniard found it hard to disavow his Church entirely – a Church whose close identification with the country over which it holds sway is not merely fortuitous. It was the Spanish Church which led the country to independence after a seven-hundred-year-old struggle – religious as much as national – against the Moslem invader, and the memory of this domestic crusade, still vivid in the minds of our Spanish contemporaries, was even more so in Goya's day.

There is a story, already referred to above, that Goya always covered the statue of the Virgin of Pilar when he embarked on the seduction of a woman in his studio. Some people have construed this as superstition, while others have seen it as symbolic of that form of courtesy which St Francis of Assisi considered to be the little sister of Charity. Whatever the truth, Goya was profoundly affected by the spirit of the Christian religion; not only towards the end of his life, when contemplation of death is normal and inevitable, but much earlier as well, if we are to judge by *Sad Presentiments of What Must Come to Pass,* the first plate of the *Disasters.* Andrès Laszlo describes it thus: 'A figure drawn naturally and in depth, recalling Christ praying on the Mount of Olives, is picked out against a sombre background in the Rembrandt manner. It is symbolic of the sufferings of the Spanish people, a prelude to the Good Friday in the history of a nation.'

PORTRAIT OF THE FRENCH AMBASSADOR GUILLEMARDET, 1798

The two Majas

Prejudices were very strong in the days when Goya painted *The Maja Nude,* especially in Spain. Echoes of the sensation it caused can still be heard in the twentieth century, principally because of an enduring (and erroneous) belief that it depicts the Duchess of Alba, and that Goya intended it as an unseemly reminder to the world at large that her body held no secrets for him. This legend seems to have stemmed from the fact that the Duchess acquired or asked to be presented with the two *Majas* as soon as they were painted. It was thought that she wanted to shield them from the public gaze for personal reasons, but she may simply have been prompted by a friendly desire to protect them from the attentions of the Inquisition, for reasons which will become plain later.

There is a story that when Alphonso XIII, the last reigning Bourbon, was being shown portraits by Velazquez and Goya of the most degenerate members of the royal family, the erstwhile Duke of Alba, who was conducting the tour of inspection, paused before each one and said emphatically: 'An ancestor of yours, Your Majesty'.

Alphonso was extremely irritated by this, but his moment came when they passed *The Maja Nude.* Turning to his companion, he remarked: 'An ancestor of yours,

Duke.' The Duke of Alba was so enraged that he promptly ordered the remains of his too-notorious ancestress to be exhumed in order to prove that she could not have been the original model – a fact which in any case emerges clearly from a comparison between Goya's numerous portraits or sketches of her and the object of scandal.

Be that as it may, when Goya painted and signed *The Maja Clothed* and *The Maja Nude* in 1800, the only acknowledged nude in the whole of Spanish painting was Velazquez's *Venus and Cupid* ('The Rokeby Venus') – and even Velazquez only escaped the wrath of the Inquisition thanks to the patronage of Philip IV, who almost certainly commissioned the picture for his own delectation.

In Goya's day any painter who depicted human nakedness was liable to punishment. Velazquez chastely portrayed his Venus from behind, using the artifice of a mirror to convey her face to the beholder, and her nude body possesses such an admirable purity of line that its sensual appeal is overlaid by a predominantly aesthetic emotion. To Goya, sensual appeal was his point of departure. Far from sublimating it, he stated it boldly. His model was slightly stocky, slightly common and built for pleasure – the sort of woman with whom he no doubt felt at ease.

Goya was at his most relaxed when painting women who appealed to him physically. Despite his natural irascibility and fits of jealousy, he was ready to forgive women any sin except that of growing old, ugly and uncongenial. As soon as he started work on a female

PORTRAIT OF THE MARQUESA DE LAS MERCEDES, 1799

PORTRAIT OF DON JAVIER GOYA ('THE MAN IN GREY'), *c.* 1798

model his brush forgot all the human imperfections it had stressed and his pen the countless terrifying masks that it had traced. His colouring became light and luminous and his brush-strokes caressed the canvas as though it were flesh.

Goya evokes the ambiguous nature of an erotic intimacy compounded of the world of sensation and the world of sensibility with a restraint which robs the subject of none of its animal quality. One cannot help feeling that he wanted to convey, through its inherent sensuality, the drama which, for better or worse, links two people united by physical desire – in this case, Goya and his *maja* of a day.

He painted her twice: once clothed, and ready to give and receive the pleasure which she awaits with a kind of serene anguish written in the fixity of her gaze and the slight twist of her lip; and once naked, still in the same pose but this time satisfied and relaxed, with her hair loose, her gaze more vacant and her mouth curved in a contented smile. It was the first time a nude had not been idealized – the first time, too, that juxtaposed expressions of different psychological or emotional 'moments' had been grafted on to the same 'real' subject observed from the same angle.

Charles IV and His Family

'Imagination bereft of Reason produces impossible monsters; united with it, it is the mother of the arts and produces marvels.' And again: 'The dream of Reason produces monsters.' Goya's commentaries on the *Caprices,* which are equally applicable to the *Disasters of War* and *Proverbs,* takes on a very special flavour when one contemplates *Charles IV and His Family.* What a masterly, admirable, horrible picture! Only Goya, with his subtle but essential brutality, could have reconciled the demands of protocol and art in this way without giving rise to gnashings of teeth or, worse still, yawns of boredom.

A few months earlier, Maria Luisa had commanded Goya to come and paint her portrait and that of the King. She was tired of seeing the fashionable painter of the day permanently under the wing of the Duchess of Alba, and Goya, who was currently embroiled with the Holy Office, found her offer of patronage far from unwelcome.

THE MIRACLE OF ST ANTHONY
(CUPOLA OF SAN ANTONIO DE LA FLORIDA), 1798

THE MIRACLE OF ST ANTHONY (DETAIL)

Having already painted most of the fourteen people who were to figure in *Charles IV and His Family* several times – adults, adolescents and children alike – the artist was intimately familiar with the features, silhouettes and characteristic poses of the royal family. He nevertheless embarked, during the early months of 1800, on a whole series of extremely forceful individual studies, some of which can now be seen grouped to good advantage round the finished picture in the Prado. Their realism – e.g. that of the sclerotic old owl's poll which represents the face of Doña Maria Josefa, the King's sister – was not toned down in the final version, and one is understandably tempted to ascribe it to mental cruelty on the part of the painter. However, the stupefaction which this collection of monsters inspires in the twentieth century observer differs little from that evinced by contemporaries who actually met Goya's principal models in the flesh.

Of Queen Maria Luisa, a woman of monumental ugliness with a belly deformed by numerous pregnancies and eyes brimming with ruthlessness, arrogance and deceit, one French ambassador wrote: 'The need to conceal the irregularities of her life from the eyes of the King for thirty years has endowed her with a propensity for extreme dissimulation. No woman lies with greater ease and assurance.'

Although the King stands one pace to the fore, in deference to protocol, Maria Luisa is strongly lit and occupies the centre of the picture – appropriately, since it was she who ruled the kingdom through the agency of Godoy, formerly one of the guards officers from whom she systematically recruited her temporary bed-fellows, and now her Prime Minister and acknowledged lover.

What of the King himself? Clad in a ceremonial costume resplendent with a firework display of decorations which Velazquez would not have disowned, the King is simply the King. He stands there in a becoming pose, left leg forward, hand on the hilt of a sword whose scabbard disappears beneath the hem of his dress-coat, deep-set eyes registering a mixture of sternness and good-nature. One can picture him playing the fool with his grooms after a drinking-session, blazing away at deer and boar put up by peasant beaters armed with sticks, signing absurd treaties with a dignified flourish and complacently telling people that his wife was the most unfortunate of women because, as Queen, she had no time to cast eyes at men who were inevitably of inferior rank and therefore unacceptable.

The royal children are adorably shy, the sons-in-law starchy, the uncles and brothers all the more solemn for being in the background, and the heir apparent in the left foreground strangely flattered by the painter, if we are to judge from a description given by his mother-in-law, the Queen of Naples: '...a ball of a man who comes up to my shoulder, all body, almost no legs, a dwarfish head... frightful of feature, a terrifying voice; an utter imbecile... The Prince does nothing, does not read, does not write, does not think – nothing. Nothing... And this is deliberate, for they want him to be an idiot.' All these figures, however nondescript, loathsome, pitiful – even congenial – they may appear to us, combine to form a sort of frieze round the bourgeois tragi-comedy of the royal couple. Confronted by such inanity, flabbiness and complacency, even Napoleon was misled. Eight years later at Bayonne, having failed to differentiate between the Spanish royal family and the Spanish people, he made one of the gravest mistakes of his career.

Here as in the *Majas,* the first 'modern' painter did not use reality as a means to express a sentiment allegoric-

THE CHURCHING, *c.* 1815

ally. He expressed that sentiment despite himself, as it were, simply by observing reality. Looking at such a picture, one is tempted to subscribe to Elie Faure's view that 'of all the great Spaniards who were subtle and savage, Goya is the most subtle, the most savage'. 'Within the context of that frightful realism which enables the Spaniards to manufacture cripples, to torture and be tortured with an indifference which the uncomprehending call cruelty, to stuff trailing entrails back into horses' bellies, Goya is the most implacable,' continues Elie Faure, who rightly regards his picture of the royal family as 'an assembly of monsters brutalized by accumulated imperfections, devout practices, furtive orgies and fear'.

This is true, but it does not go far enough. In fact, it is not cruelty which makes the Spaniard 'stuff trailing entrails' back into the bellies of horses involved in the ritual of the bullfight, but the fact that tradition wills it so, and that no one can do otherwise without testifying to an unseemly and, thus, reprehensible imagination.

Similarly, it was not cruelty that prompted Goya to endow the members of Charles IV's family with faces which almost make the 'ferocious' countenances recorded in Velazquez's portraits of Philip III's family seem models of purity and intelligence by comparison. He did so because he could not evade the golden rule of 'frightful realism' which Elie Faure defines so well. Was Goya aware that he had complied with this rule? To a degree – yes, since he did all he could to mitigate the fact, happily without affecting the final result.

It would be very wrong to credit the painter of *Charles IV and His Family* with a wish to caricature. On the contrary, he went to considerable lengths to humanize the whole scene by bathing the disturbing veracity of his figures in a symphony of grey, red and blue light. What is more, his models proclaimed their collective delight and satisfaction at having been so faithfully portrayed in such distinguished company. As for Goya himself, it is inconceivable that he would ever have dared to poke fun at such important people if they had not been convinced of their unrivalled beauty.

Almost simultaneously Goya's services were enlisted by Godoy, who had not figured in the family portrait. The favourite had himself painted in great state in his Aranjuez residence, which was connected with the royal apartments by a private passage. Goya took advantage of his visit to paint a portrait, overwhelming in its charm and delicacy, of the sad and gentle little 'Princess of the Peace', Countess of Chinchon and daughter of the Infante Don Luis, whom Queen Maria Luisa had forced to marry her lover.

In one of his last letters to Zapater, the painter speaks in glowing terms of his stay and of the kindness heaped upon him by the all-powerful Godoy: 'He desired me to keep my cloak on for dinner... He has done all he can to be agreeable, he has taken me for a drive in his carriage with the greatest protestations of friendship imaginable.' Just as he had proclaimed at the time of his initial successes: 'These princes are angels!', so now, in the midst of his bragging, he took the same naive precautions as he had done in the old days. 'Here,' he told Zapater, 'is a letter which proves it (the esteem in which Godoy held him); I do not know if you will be able to read his writing, which is worse than mine... Do not show it to anyone, say nothing about it, and return it to me.'

The writer of such a letter could never have been capable of secretly ridiculing the royal personages whose portraits he was privileged to paint, but then Goya was not the first or last intelligent man to have been so fascinated by wealth and power as to lose all capacity for criticism. Fortunately his eye was quicker than his intellect.

Before the storm

Maria Teresa, thirteenth Duchess of Alba, died under
mysterious circumstances on 28 July 1802. She had
been struck down by an illness some days earlier, and
never regained consciousness. Her death was so sudden
and unexpected that there was an immediate suspicion
that she had been poisoned, either because of the Queen's
jealousy or as a precautionary measure by Godoy, who
was convinced that the Duchess had been plotting his
downfall and seducing his ministers to that end. A letter
from him to Maria Luisa had explicitly stated that 'the
Alba woman and all her supporters ought to be buried
in a vast pit'.

Whether due to foul play or not, the demise of the
principal object of Godoy's hatred and the Queen's
jealousy was now an accomplished fact. Even in death,
however, Maria Teresa flouted convention twice by

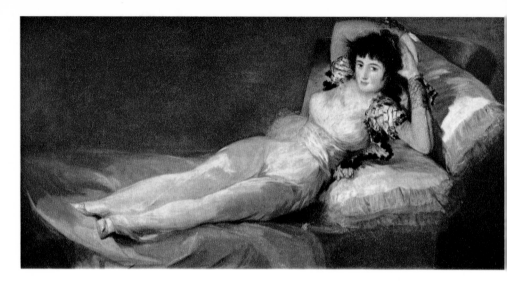

causing two sensations: her manner of dying and her last will and testament.

When her funeral had been held – promptly and *in secreto* in view of the circumstances – it was learned that she had cast the whole of her immense fortune to the four winds of charity. The pretty, autocratic and capricious woman had forgotten neither the least of her friends nor the humblest of her innumerable servants. Legacy by legacy, annuity by annuity, everything was distributed among them. Among those who fared particularly well were the children of her friends and the foundlings who were fed in her servants' halls. Goya's son Javier received an annuity of three thousand five hundred *reales* in addition to the twelve thousand which his father had obtained for him from Charles IV when he presented the plates of the *Caprices* to the Royal Collections three years before.

THE MAJA NUDE, *c*. 1798-1800

Quite as agitated by the Duchess's generosity as he was by the whispered comments on her death, the King ordered an inquiry to be held under Godoy's auspices. The humble beneficiaries of the will made ideal suspects. Some of them were thrown into prison and others discharged, and the will was invalidated. No one was surprised when Queen Maria Luisa appeared shortly afterwards exultantly wearing her late rival's finest jewels, nor when, later on, Godoy's effects were found to include some of the Duchess's best Goyas, among them *The Maja Clothed* and *The Maja Nude*.

The sordid tragi-comedy which was enacted after her untimely death merely confirms and underlines the fact that the most vivacious, charming, impudent, generous and – when all is said and done – the greatest lady of the eighteenth century could not, and might not have wished to, outlive the age which she typified to such perfection.

It is true that Goya grumbled at her, notably in the *Caprices,* one of which depicts the Duchess and a bull-fighter cooing together on a branch while the painter, also in the guise of a bird, surveys them with a sad and jaundiced eye. He not only grumbled at her infidelities but – which was far less gentlemanly – often committed 'indiscretions' calculated to suggest the nature of the relationship between the Duchess and himself. On the latter point, some people have read a desire for publicity into one of the most famous passages in his correspondence with Zapater. 'You would have done better to come and help me paint the Alba woman, who came to my studio yesterday so that I could paint her face for her; I certainly find it more agreeable than painting canvas.' Apart from the fact that this letter is, with equal probability, dated 1794 by some and 1800 by others, it was fashionable at this period for ladies of the nobility to have their faces made up occasionally by their favourite painter, so the passage in question hardly constitutes proof of intimacy or an avowal of the same.

It is equally certain, however, that despite his jealousies, sulks and fits of temper, Goya regarded the Duchess of Alba as something far more than a patroness and occasional mistress. His vanity was titillated by her great name and his sensuality by her beauty, but he also took a bitter-sweet pleasure in the fact that she seemed, frivolity and all, to symbolize the youth whose loss haunted him more and more cruelly as time went by. Her blend of *grande dame* and girlishness made her, in all probability, the only woman who ever inspired this vigorous and sensual man with genuine love. The depth of his attachment to her may be gauged from his behaviour after that fateful day in July 1802. Haggard and depressed, aggressive and bitter, he virtually abandoned his studio and roamed aimlessly through the streets, immersing himself in the solitude of the deaf. His gloom and despair remained with him always.

He showed scant reaction in 1804 when the Academy elected his mediocre but persevering rival Gregorio Ferro to the vacant post of Director-General by twenty-nine votes to eight. In less than ten years, Goya had produced ten or more masterpieces which had put him on a par with the greatest names in the history of painting. Was the genius that had been so feverishly exploited on the wane? This seems to have been the general view, and people who had not yet had their portraits painted by him were disconsolate when he turned their commissions down. Believing him to be a doomed man, they were afraid that their last chance to sit for him would soon be gone. Goya, whose mind was elsewhere, neither worried about this nor sought to revive his flagging inspiration.

In fact, the times were hardly conducive to this. Soon after the Duchess of Alba had been laid in her tomb the storm-clouds which were hemming Spain in on every side, studiously ignored by everyone, began to loom ever darker above the peninsula itself.

In 1803 Napoleon Bonaparte bared his teeth. He wanted Spain to take a more active part in the war against England and he needed money. Godoy was characteristically evasive, but Napoleon retorted by demanding

CHARLES IV AND HIS FAMILY (DETAIL), 1800

PORTRAIT OF DOÑA MARIA JOSEFA (SISTER OF CHARLES IV), *c.* 1800

PORTRAIT OF THE INFANTE DON FRANCISCO DE PAULA ANTONIO
(BROTHER OF CHARLES IV), c. 1800

his head, and sent Charles IV a letter in which he crudely
revealed the favourite's role in the bosom of the royal
family. Whether or not Charles IV read this letter when
the French ambassador handed it to him, Spain yielded
to Napoleon's arbitrary demands. The year 1803 also
marked the active invasion of Spanish hearts and minds
by political chaos. Hitherto, unrest had been confined
to an intellectual *élite* with an extremely limited radius
of action. From now on, the whole country was swept
by two currents of emotion: on the one hand, profound
national resentment at the increasing extent and blatancy
of French pressure, and, on the other, a no less profound
yearning to utilize Napoleon's prestige – and even his
armies – in a bid to slough off the nepotism of that

strange *ménage à trois,* Charles IV, Maria Luisa and Godoy. It is difficult to follow the course of events unless one grasps the fact that, from now on, these two currents were complementary rather than contradictory.

With the advent of 1804, financial collapse and anarchy were joined by plague and famine. 'The year 1804,' Godoy wrote in his memoirs, 'brought new misfortunes and alarming phenomena everywhere. The order of the seasons was reversed, the earth quaked... People thought they saw a rain of blood, rivers left their beds, communities were drowned and engulfed...' 1805 brought a lull, but only in Goya's private life. He settled some money on his son Javier and married him to Doña Gumersinda, daughter of Don Julian Martin de Goicoechea, a prominent citizen of Zaragoza.

By 1807 things had gone from bad to worse and confusion reigned supreme. After blustering at Napoleon, Godoy was now secretly negotiating with him. As a reward for his good offices, a small kingdom was to be carved out of Portugal for him by the French army. Godoy, who was naive enough to believe Napoleon's promises, promptly commissioned Goya to produce an official portrait which depicted him as a sort of monarch in the field with his army. While he was still negotiating, however, a plot was hatched against him at the Spanish Court. The heir to the throne, whom Godoy, abetted by the Queen, had tried to oust by every possible means, not excluding systematic brutalization, suddenly rebelled. On the advice of friends, he wrote a letter informing the King of his wife's marital infidelities and of her lover's political double-dealing. It is not clear whether Charles IV read this letter either, but Maria Luisa and Godoy reacted swiftly. Placed under surveillance, the future Ferdinand VII broke down, confessed everything his enemies wanted him to confess, grovelled, begged forgiveness, and denounced all his friends.

At the very moment when the Infante Ferdinand's mockery of a trial was taking place, French troops crossed the frontier under Junot. A wave of hope surged through Spain. No one believed that the French forces had come as anything but friends. Even Godoy preened himself on what he regarded as a prompt token of Napoleon's determination to implement the treaty he had just signed with him, but the people interpreted it differently. In their eyes, the French troops were there for only one reason: to help them get rid of Godoy.

On 17 March the mob burst into the Prime Minister's palace and sacked it. On 23 March Murat entered Madrid in triumph. Meanwhile, Charles IV had hurriedly abdicated and Ferdinand had emerged from prison to put Godoy in irons and assume the crown.

What of Goya during these troubled years? Not having touched a brush or pencil for many months after the Duchess of Alba's death, he gradually set to work once more, unenthusiastically and without haste. Thanks to the very high fees he charged, three or four portraits a year were enough to guarantee him a decent living. He painted them – usually in less than a day – without conviction and to order, as in former days: neo-Classical or in the English manner, according to his client's wishes.

SELF-PORTRAIT IN A TALL HAT, *c.* 1800

This became so well known that one prospective client begged a mutual friend to persuade Goya to paint his portrait 'as he does when he wants to'. It was a vain precaution. The portrait in question, that of the naval historian Don José Vargas y Ponce, turned out to be 'standard Goya' – neither better nor worse than the others. No one thought of complaining, since the

SELF-PORTRAIT, 1799

painter maintained a reign of terror in his studio. 'All visitors were kept out of the way,' recounts an eyewitness, 'and if a close friend were present he had to stay motionless in a corner. The model became a martyr who could not twitch an eyebrow or stretch a weary limb. At the slightest infringement, Goya would fly into a rage and hurl his palette aside.'

For all that, he occasionally made an effort where friends were concerned, especially women whose physical appearance inspired him. The portraits of Doña Isabel Cobos de Porcel (1806) and Doña Antonia Zarate (1807) are among the finest he ever painted; the first, which is in the National Gallery, because of its radiant, carnal exuberance, and the second, now in New York, because of its melancholy charm of expression, a blend of eighteenth-century gaiety and grace and nineteenth-century gravity.

These were exceptions, however. Apart from six wooden panels illustrating the exploits and ultimate fate of El Maragoto, one of the most notorious of the innumerable bandits of the period, painted in 1806 and reminiscent of the forgotten style of *Carnival Scene*, Goya's only respite from stiff conventional portraits consisted in drawing what he saw by chance while out walking; and what his eye retained, for the most part, was the sight of beggars and grotesques, wretchedness and stupidity. Goya was sixty-two now. Gloomy, embittered and unsociable, he abandoned himself to the sullen joys of waiting, convinced that there was nothing left to wait for. It was almost as if he were deliberately striving to achieve oblivion.

The Spanish people welcomed Napoleon's armies and acclaimed their new king as '*el rey idolatrado*' because of his hatred for Godoy, but the short-lived sense of deliverance which pervaded Spain at the close of 1807 found no echo in Goya's work.

PART THREE:
CHAOS, SOLITUDE AND GLORY (1808-1828)

The Second of May

Madrid, 2 May 1808. The rattle of musketry could be heard everywhere. A few isolated shots followed by bursts of sustained firing indicated that French troops were trying to dislodge some insurgents. A battle that had started with stones and stilettos was now being waged with muskets and cannon procured from Spanish regiments, which had broken out of the barracks where they had been confined. Muffled volleys rang out in the tightly shuttered streets, followed immediately by the deafening hubbub of a mob put to flight by a cavalry charge.

Amid the booming of cannon, crackle of musket-fire and confused din made by stampeding men and horses, cries rent the smoke-filled air – cries of mortal hatred uttered not only in Castilian but also in Polish, French, German and Arabic. Napoleon Bonaparte had recruited

PORTRAIT OF MANUEL GODOY, 1800-1801

or levied men from every land that lay in his path. By evening of the same sanguinary day, quiet reigned throughout the city, broken only by the volleys of firing-squads at work.

One man – Goya, the deaf painter – had heard nothing of the tragic cacophony around him, but he had seen the Mamelukes – so like the Moorish troops who had occupied his country for seven centuries – hacking away with their sabres at the bodies and faces of hundreds of humble Madrileños like the ones he had painted with such fervour on the dome of San Antonio ten years before. When night came and all was quiet again save for the spine-chilling sound of the firing-squads which

PORTRAIT OF QUEEN MARIA LUISA, *c.* 1800

he could not hear, his gardener came, lantern in hand, to guide him through streets littered with wounded, dead and dying to the Puerta del Sol and the Prado, from now on sacred to the memory of the insurgents who had been ruthlessly slaughtered there by the foreign soldiery. There were so many of them that executions continued until the evening of the following day, 3 May.

The vision of Goya guided through this carnage by a gardener carrying a lantern may well be apocryphal. It is more than probable, however, that he witnessed at least some of the more terrible features of the uprising, which – according to contemporary reports – cost the lives of 'five persons of liberal occupation and two men of quality' as well as an unspecified number of workers, servants, shop-keepers and women of the lower classes. In reality, hundreds died, and a rift opened between Spain and France which it took many years to heal.

To men like Goya, liberals who had pinned all their hopes on France, it had been a brutal and incomprehensible blow. This was one of the main reasons why Goya did not paint *The Charge of the Mamelukes* ('The Second of May') and *The Execution of the Defenders of Madrid* ('The Third of May') – of which more will be said later – until six years afterwards (1814), by which time French troops had left Spanish territory.

Horror among the liberals was matched by comparative satisfaction in conservative circles. Don Antonio, President of the Junta and the man whose round, stern, placid face peers over his royal brother's shoulder in *Charles IV and His Family*, neatly expressed this sentiment to Murat on the evening of 2 May: 'We are delighted at what has happened. People will no longer come and tell us that an army can be annihilated by peasants armed with sticks and knives. Everyone has at last been convinced that one battalion of regular troops is enough to disperse ten thousand of them.'

However, Don Antonio, and Don Fransisco de Paula Antonio were the last remaining male representatives of the royal family in Madrid. Charles IV, Maria Luisa and Godoy were in the process of taking orders from Napoleon at Bayonne, whither Ferdinand VII had also been summoned, only to be informed by the master of Europe that he did not in any way consider him to be the King of Spain. Napoleon had already decided to install one of his brothers on the throne instead.

Although no news of what was going on in Bayonne had penetrated the Pyrenees, vague presentiments of disaster prompted the people to take up arms on behalf of *their* royal family. At the frontier, peasants had rushed forward to cut the traces of Ferdinand's coach and dissuade him from going further. At Madrid, it had been a child's tears which sparked off the revolt. 'The *Infantido* does not want to leave. They are kidnapping him!' The rumour spread like wildfire among the crowds who were watching preparations for a long journey in the courtyard of the Royal Palace. A French officer presented himself at the gates on a routine diplomatic mission at the very moment when the over-excited mob hurled itself at the horses of the Infantido's coach and unharnessed them from their shafts. The French officer's presence

PORTRAIT OF DR PERAL, *c.* 1800

added fuel to the flames. Seizing upon him as a convenient scapegoat, the mob attacked him. Soldiers came to his assistance and shots rang out on both sides. From then on, the insurrection and massacres of 2 May were inevitable.

It was ironical that the uprising should have been linked with the departure of Don Antonio, who later rejoiced at its bloody suppression, and Don Fransisco de Paula Antonio, whom everyone but the crowed knew to be the natural son of Godoy, the man they execrated and had hounded out of office.

The events of 2 May interrupted Goya's efforts to finish an equestrian portrait of Ferdinand VII. He was indignant because the new king, too busy consolidating his reputation as *'el rey idolatrado'* by distributing money in the suburbs of Madrid, lowering the price of tobacco and issuing permits to hunt in the royal parks, had only granted him two forty-five-minute sittings – 'insufficient,' Goya declared, 'for the painting of a good picture, as opposed to a portrait for a special occasion'.

The painter's ill-humour is surprising when one reflects that he had often reiterated, and was to do so again, that 'anyone who aspires to the name of painter must be capable of reproducing from memory, with brush or pencil, each scene or incident in all its essential features, after seeing it once.'

PORTRAIT OF DOÑA ISABEL COBOS DE PORCEL, *c.* 1806

PORTRAIT OF DOÑA TERESA SUREDA, *c.* 1805

The cancer spreads

What had occurred to make the situation deteriorate so rapidly? On 23 March 1808 Murat had entered a rejoicing city in triumph, Ferdinand VII had donned the crown amid universal acclaim and Napoleon was still sending his army repeated admonitions to tread carefully: 'If war breaks out, all will be lost.'

By 1 April, however, Murat was anxiously considering a ban on all public assemblies in the Spanish capital. He was alarmed by signs of popular unrest. One of his aides-de-camp had run a nocturnal assailant through with his sword and had been pursued by a mob of passers-by bent on lynching him. A Madrileño had hurled himself, stiletto in hand, at an officer escorted by two soldiers. When arrested, he calmly confessed that he had been 'suddenly inspired to kill three Frenchmen'.

Napoleon, who described Murat in his *Mémorial* as 'a hero but a beast', did not take his brother-in-law's fears too seriously. In his eyes, 2 May was merely an abortive insurrection which had been satisfactorily crushed. His ambitions were too lofty for him to spare a thought for the reactions of what he regarded as the '*canaille*' of Madrid. 'In the battle of new ideas,' he wrote at St Helena, 'in the century's great march against the old Europe, I could not allow Spain to lag behind in social reorganization. It was absolutely essential to involve her, willy-nilly, in the French movement.'

Personal contact with the royal personages whom we know from Goya's great picture was hardly calculated to aid the Emperor's understanding of Spanish problems.

DISASTERS OF WAR: 'WHAT COURAGE!', 1810

Having assembled them at Bayonne, Napoleon found himself confronted by a portly, flabby, conceited nobody of a king who whined when deprived of 'his' Godoy because he never dared open his mouth in his absence, and a queen whose mind was even more monstrously vulgar and hideous than her body. The former was mainly interested in knowing whether the forests in his appointed place of exile would be adequately stocked with game, and the latter's one concern was to vent her spleen upon the son who had dared to come between her and Godoy. She even went so far as to demand the guillotine for him, and addressed him publicly as 'bastard' when he baulked at handing over his crown to the French. As for the stubborn and oafish target of her wrath, who had allowed himself to become enmeshed in an affair which was, to quote Barante, 'conducted like an intrigue and concluded like an ambush', Napoleon dismissed him with some justification as an 'extremely stupid and evil' creature.

Under such circumstances, Napoleon could have had few scruples with regard to the royal family and precious little respect for a nation which allowed itself to be led and represented by such people. 'Spain can no longer be saved except by Napoleon', he dictated to Charles IV, and Charles IV duly appended his royal signature.

When Joseph Bonaparte mounted the Bourbon throne – which had previously been declined by his brother Louis – even Ferdinand VII abandoned all resistance, at least outwardly. 'Sire,' he wrote to Napoleon, 'I offer Your Imperial and Royal Majesty my most heartfelt compliments on the satisfaction Your Majesty has had in the installation of Your Majesty's beloved brother on the throne of Spain. The object of all our desires having ever been the happiness of the noble nation which inhabits this vast kingdom, we could not see at its head a monarch so worthy and so fitted by his virtues to assure the same without deriving the greatest consolation therefrom.'

The full humour and irony of this missive, which betrays the influence of Canon Escoiquita, Ferdinand's chief adviser, can only be appreciated if it is seen in its

proper context. The contrast between official pronouncements and the realities of the situation is perfectly illus-
trated by the fact that three days after the insurrection
of 2 May Napoleon formally renounced all claims on Spain
and the West Indies; on the thirty-first of the same month
he issued his famous proclamation: 'Spaniards, your
nation was perishing after a long death-agony. I have
seen your ills; I am going to bring you the remedy for
them. Your monarchy is old; my mission is to rejuvenate
it... I shall set your glorious crown on the head of one
who is another myself.'

Having safely arrived in the capital on 21 July, Joseph
was compelled to leave again nine days later because
his safety could no longer be guaranteed. The country
was swarming with thousands of guerilla bands who
harried the French army on every side, sabotaged its
supply lines and engaged it – often with success – in
pitched battle.

Joseph had scarcely departed when a horde of ragged
but triumphant *guerilleros* entered Madrid. Goya hurriedly
completed and delivered his equestrian portrait of Ferdinand VII, refusing to accept payment. His model,
by this time a prisoner in the Château de Valençay, had
just been proclaimed king for the second time at Madrid,
where, thanks to Goya, he at least reigned in effigy.
Popular rejoicing knew no bounds. It persisted until
Napoleon's armies returned four months later.

It is tempting to credit the events of 2 May 1808 with
having provided the psychological 'shock' which roused

DISASTERS OF WAR: 'WHY?', 1810

Goya from the sort of torpor which had overcome him after the Duchess of Alba's death in 1802. That it came as a shock goes without saying, but its effect on him was somewhat delayed.

When the tattered *guerilleros* paraded through the streets after Joseph Bonaparte's first and fleeting appearance in Madrid, Goya was among the first to subscribe to their 'war chest'. This did not deter him, once Joseph had returned on a more stable footing, from presiding with two other painters, Napoli and Maëlla, over the selection of fifty of the best Spanish paintings for despatch to Paris at Napoleon's command, to wit, three works by Velazquez,

DISASTERS OF WAR: 'THEY WILL NOT ARRIVE IN TIME', 1810

two by Murillo, four by Ribera and five by Zurbarán, the balance being of lesser merit; nor from zealously painting portraits of the leading lights of the new regime, King Joseph included; nor from accepting the 'Red Cravat of the Order of Spain', awarded by the French to their most loyal collaborators and scornfully christened 'the aubergine' by the Spaniards.

It is true that the prevailing complexity of events and extreme confusion of interests often evoked strangely perverse reactions in different people. On the one hand, Charles IV's brother had congratulated Murat on putting down a revolt whose sole aim was to preserve the Bourbon throne. On the other, most of the liberal and patriotic 'intelligentsia' rejoiced at a foreign occupation which they hoped would carry out the reforms which they had so long awaited in vain. In fact, once he had firmly established Joseph at Madrid, Napoleon did fulfil the liberals' hopes by suppressing at one stroke, on 4 December 1808, the tribunals of the Inquisition, feudal rights, provincial excise duties, seigneurial courts of law, the Council of Castile and two-thirds of all religious houses.

The traditionalists protested furiously at this, as did the hidebound and uneducated masses, who stubbornly preferred honourable servitude to freedom imposed by foreigners. Among the few intellectuals who ranged themselves with the people was Gaspar Melchior de Jovellanos, who joined the Junta of Cadiz to help organize the war of liberation. When friends who were also friends of Goya castigated Jovellanos for having made common cause with 'reactionaries', his response was a model of courage, common sense and integrity: 'I do not belong to a party, but to the sacred cause of the independence of my fatherland... Can Joseph apply the noble principles of a "philosopher king" in a country ravaged by foreign soldiers?'

In 1810, two years after the 2 May insurrection and in a country still 'ravaged by foreign soldiers', Goya started work on his first etchings for the *Disasters of War*.

The Disasters of War

It was not until 1820 that Ceán Bermúdez assembled
the eighty-five plates comprising the 'Fatal Consequences
of the Sanguinary War with Bonaparte in Spain, and
Other Emphatic Caprices', as Goya intended to call the
series of etchings which he had begun to engrave in 1810.
It was not until 1863, or thirty-five years after the artist's
death, that the Academy of San Fernando published them
under the title *Disasters of War,* having previously eliminated *The Prisoners,* three etchings which it considered
to be unrelated to the main group but which Goya may

have intended as an epilogue to his terrible pictorial narrative.

The *Disasters* defy comparison with any work of the same genre before or since, with the possible exception of Picasso's *Sueño y Mentira de Franco* and the frenzied pen-drawings which he made while engaged on *Guernica* – his own personal *Charge of the Mamelukes* – during the other Spanish war of which he was, like Goya a century-and-a-half before him, if not a protagonist at least an inspired illustrator.

DISASTERS OF WAR: 'THIS IS WORSE', 1810

On the one hand, the nationalist Junta: 'All inhabitants are authorized to arm themselves in order to attack and despoil French soldiers.' On the other, the army of occupation: 'Anyone taken carrying arms will be hanged without further formality.'

'There is no remedy,' Goya wrote beneath the fifteenth etching of the *Disasters,* which depicts one execution among many.

Clusters of corpses rotting by the roadside, women raped, soldiers butchered, towns and villages sacked, epidemics, famine, shootings, hangings – it was the same dreary story for years on end. The first man to stand up to Napoleon successfully was a nameless individual whose unassuming sobriquet was 'El Incognito' (The Unknown). The alcalde of a village near Seville, he began by recruiting his four brothers, twelve peasant friends and eight soldiers. Several days later a group of smugglers joined his banner, and by the time he offered his force to the Supreme Junta it numbered nine thousand trained men. As soon as Joseph Bonaparte came into contact with the country which had bred El Incognito and his ilk, all his illusions vanished. 'I believe,' he said to General Savary, 'that there is not even one neutral in Spain, and that all are against us. This is understandable. In France the Revolution was made by the French and enjoyed wide support; here it pleases no one, has no supporters and, what is more, has been made by foreigners. Everyone takes up arms at the very name.' At the time of his first lamentable entry into Madrid, Joseph wrote to the Emperor himself: 'I have as my enemy a nation twelve million strong, courageous and exasperated in the extreme. The honest men are no more for me than the rogues. No, Sire, you are mistaken; your glory will be ruined in Spain.'

But it was already too late. At Baylen in the foothills of the Sierra Morena, between the Rumblar and Guadiela and on the road from Cordova to Madrid, seven thousand French soldiers under General Dupont were forced to surrender their arms to General Castanos and a scratch force of twenty-five thousand Andalusian peasants armed with pitchforks, flails and scythes.

While Castanos thought that 'Heaven had sent him a dream', Napoleon's reaction to the news of his first defeat – coming, as it did, at a time when he needed all his prestige if he were to retain control over his too-vast and too-swiftly-conquered empire – was to describe Dupont's surrender at Baylen as 'one of the most extraordinary acts of ineptitude and stupidity imaginable'. He could not afford to take defeat lying down and allow English troops to establish themselves in Spain, so he assumed personal command of his armies, forced the supposedly impregnable passes held by the Spaniards and brought Joseph back to Madrid.

'He painted very far away from his sitter, capturing masses and effects, natural aspects and attitudes, never concerning himself with features and contours.'

What Goya's contemporaries said of his portrait technique applied even more strongly when his subjects ceased to be isolated individuals or groups and became a collective

THE MARTYRDOM OF SS JEAN DE BREBEUF AND GABRIEL LALLEMANT, *c.* 1815

phenomenon like the war of liberation. It would be rewarding if one could assemble in a single exhibition all the drawings, etchings and paintings – from the preliminary red chalk sketches for the *Disasters* to *The Execution of the Defenders of Madrid* – which Goya devoted to the tragic war into which his country had been plunged. Apart from the immense historical value of such an exhibition, it would establish not only that Goya ushered in one of the main trends in modern painting between 1808 and 1814, but also, on a more general plane, that he was one of the first exponents of an essentially modern intellectual and emotional approach.

A slightly later work which might be included in this group is *The Martyrdom of SS Jean de Brébeuf and Gabriel Lallemant,* which depicts the murder of the Archbishop of Quebec and the consumption of his remains by cannibalistic Iroquois Indians. Although the theme had no connection with the Spanish war of independence, Goya's attention was obviously attracted by its horrific quality. What had happened in the forests of Quebec could equally have occurred in the sierras.

In Western conceptions of graphic and literary art, the anonymous crowd had hitherto played only a decorative role. It framed, justified and exalted the presence and existence of individualized heroes. In addition, it was sometimes called upon to play an informative role, as in the case of cathedral cornices and details of pre-Renaissance frescos, pictures by Le Nain and the Dutch School or Jacques Callot's engravings, which, like contemporary news photographs, convey the mood of a crowd at a given time and place.

Although Goya paid particular attention to the laws of decoration and the requirements of information, he went far beyond the bounds of either. When he painted a crowd without concentrating on 'features and contours' so as to capture 'masses and effects', the crowd itself became his subject and model – a personality in its own right, endowed with a soul, body and face of its own.

A soul: like the heart, suffering and expectation have reasons of which Reason knows not. The eighty-five *Disasters* and the other works which supplement them are essentially a long series of inquiries into the basis

DISASTERS OF WAR: 'WITH REASON OR WITHOUT', 1810

of these obscure reasons, which are unaffected by considerations of self-interest, logic or mortality.

A body: this teeming mass of human forms was soon to merge, in Goya's vision, into the single *Colossus* which he depicted looming above the horizon of an unknown land, its massive torso half-submerged in a mysterious night sky which suggests both the end and the creation of the world.

A face: there is a gearing down of the constant alternation between stupidity and irony, malevolence, frivolity, goodness, intelligence and conceit, varying measures of which are to be found in each of Goya's portraits. His countless faces convey the ambiguity of all incarnate psychology; but, to the extent that the *Disasters* capture and stabilize this infinite ambiguity against a background of elemental fear, they become a single face.

Since war is simply a nonsensical hastening of death, it enabled Goya to pose the one problem that always haunted him: that of death itself.

If we have ventured far beyond the scope of decoration and information, we have also overstepped the bounds of 'commitment', the theory so enthusiastically proclaimed – and sometimes even practised – by artists and writers of the mid-twentieth century. Restating the problem in contemporary terms, André Malraux is perfectly correct in his belief that 'like the work of a duped friend as well as a bitter patriot' the *Disasters* resemble 'the sketch-book of a Communist after the occupation of his country by Russian troops'.

It would be absurd to pretend that Goya was not prompted to 'take sides' in the *Disasters* by specific political circumstances, even though his 'commitment' (a strictly private phenomenon in his day) did not contribute to the defence and glorification of the Spanish people until long after the fighting was over. However, Goya endowed the conflict with meaning and engraved it once and for all on the minds of the world at large. It was through him, rather than through eye-witness accounts and historical analyses, that posterity was to draw the appropriate moral. Goya may have been committed, but his commitment was non-systematic, semi-involuntary and retroactive.

When painting the mountain of Sainte-Victoire, Cézanne had not the least intention of involving himself in scholarly controversies over the formation of the earth's crust nor in arguments between hydro-electric dam-builders whose job it is to utilize that crust for economic or social purposes. Cézanne painted Sainte-Victoire as he saw it, and painted it in such a way that no scholar, economist or sociologist who has once beheld his painting can see the mountain other than in terms of the bluish slopes in which he clothed it. To a degree, the same applies to Goya's pictures of humble folk involved in the war of independence, but his subject was vaster, more mobile and less rewarding.

Goya spent the year 1809 in Aragón, travelling the deserted highways in his richly appointed Court Painter's carriage. French troops politely allowed him to pass because he was painter to King Joseph Bonaparte. *Guerilleros* greeted him with equal respect because he was painter to the legitimate royal family for whose reinstatement they were fighting.

During the second siege of Zaragoza, Napoleon's soldiers burst into the bedroom of General Palafox, the Aragonese resistance hero of whom Goya later painted a triumphal equestrian portrait. There, they slashed furiously with their sabres at the drawing Goya had made of the devastation caused by the earlier French bombardment. A portrait of Maria Agustina, the city's Joan of Arc, also met its end in this way.

This did not deter the painter, while still in Aragón, from agreeing to paint a portrait of King Joseph – 'from

DISASTERS OF WAR: 'THE CARNIVOROUS VULTURE', 1810

DISASTERS OF WAR: 'BURY THEM AND BE SILENT', 1810

a print', as he later explained in self-justification. The portrait was commissioned by Don Tadeo Bravo del Rivero, *Regidor* of Madrid, whose house Goya had helped to decorate on the occasion of King Joseph's first departure from the Spanish capital. According to

DISASTERS OF WAR: 'BURY THEM AND BE SILENT', 1810

Antonina Vallentin, this controversial portrait once appeared on the marble plaque supported by winged spirits in the centre of Goya's *Allegory of the City of Madrid*. In 1814 it was replaced by the word '*Constitucion*', which soon disappeared in its turn to make room for a portrait of Ferdinand VII. The monarch's features were still later replaced by a portrayal of the Book of the Constitution.

Don Tadeo was now one of the leading '*afrancesados*', as were Leandro de Moratin, who accepted the post of Royal Librarian, Melendez Valdez, Juan Antonio Llorente, ex-Secretary of the Inquisition tribunal at Madrid and an unfrocked canon, and Bernardo Yriarte, who had negotiated the surrender of Madrid with Napoleon on 2 December 1808. All were friends of Goya and all sat for him.

At the same period, a young boy was fleeing from Spain with his mother. At the gates of Vittoria, he caught sight of 'a cross to which were nailed limbs of a young man who had been hacked to pieces. Someone had had the horrible intention of rearranging the pieces and reconstructing a corpse out of the remains. The body belonged to the brother of Mina *(A Spanish Partisan)*, taken by the French. The carriage passed quite close, and the children jumped back so as not to be splashed by drops of blood.'

These few lines, which might have been a commentary on one of Goya's *Disasters,* were written by Victor Hugo. His father, General Hugo, had distinguished himself by worsting a famous Neapolitan bandit named Fra Diavolo, and had been appointed governor of Guadalajara, stamping-ground of the rebel leader El Empecinado ('the pitchy' or 'stubborn one', so nicknamed because his father was a cobbler). As a child, Victor Hugo was deeply impressed by this world of sanguinary confusion, where whole

THE CHARGE OF THE MAMELUKES ('THE SECOND OF MAY, 1808'), 1814

communities were massacred and where the rules demanded the lives of four French officers for that of one Spaniard. As an adult, Goya was no less affected, but his sense of integrity and his understanding of the tragic story elevated his treatment of it to universal heights. Fascinated by the satanic legends which he had so often evoked on canvas, the painter suddenly found himself at grips with a world of reality in which the Devil played his part without having to don the guise of a lewd and unsavoury he-goat. He was the frenzy which inspired the mob, the fear which froze the victim's heart, the loathsome brutality which prompted the soldier to butcher unarmed civilians.

What is this power in man that drives him to self-destruction? This question could serve as a commentary on all the *Disasters*. It was not prudence that made Goya dress his murderous soldiers in uniforms which only vaguely resembled those of the French invaders. To him, this was much more than a local affair. So far from being simply a partisan war-cry, the *Disasters* seem more like an indictment of prejudice. Goya begrudged hatred its existence and its capacity for compelling hatred in himself. His deafness protected him from the facile argu-

DISASTERS OF WAR: 'TO THE CEMETERY'

ments which would no doubt have been showered on him from various quarters, and he could not luxuriate in the sense of unanimity which reigns among supporters – successful or otherwise – of a 'just cause'.

It was at the precise moment when all his biographers declare him to have 'identified himself with the fate of his country' that Goya embarked on his own great adventure, the adventure of a solitary colossus in a crowd.

EXECUTION OF THE DEFENDERS OF MADRID ('THE THIRD OF MAY 1808'), 1814

The Second and Third of May - six years later

Yet another event contributed to Goya's isolation during these troubled years. His wife Josefa died in June 1812. This severed the last link with the ambitious young painter he had once been, and the distress he felt impelled him to take stock of himself. His bereavement seemed as great a threat as the uncertainty of the events which were unfolding around him.

He decided to give his son Javier some of his own paintings which he had retained because, Javier wrote later, 'he preferred them in that they had been painted in complete freedom, as his spirit willed'. It is interesting to note which pictures were involved. Among those which may be quoted with certainty are *The Colossus*, or *Panic*, the scenes depicting the career of the bandit Maragoto, some genre pictures, twelve illustrations of the horrors of war and the *Majas on the Balcony* – probably the one painted in 1810. (Goya often returned to this theme – two women leaning over a balcony with the silhouettes of men in sombreros in the background – and by 1820 his handling of the subject had acquired unrivalled freedom and mastery.) Foremost among the pictures which the painter kept in his possession were *Portrait of Pedro Romero* and his portrait of the Duchess of Alba wearing a ring inscribed with his own name.

In January 1812, while Napoleon was mustering his armies for the Russian campaign, the future Duke of Wellington launched an offensive aimed at Madrid. Joseph Bonaparte left there in August, before the arrival of the English forces. Wellington remained in the capital barely long enough to hear the delirious crowds chanting 'Y viva la Nación! Y viva Velinton!' to watch a parade by *guerilleros* such as El Empecinado and El Medico – whose appearance perturbed him a little – and to have his portrait painted by Goya. It was by now a firmly established tradition that, whatever changes occurred in the government or political situation, Goya always made a portrait of the victor of the moment.

Joseph, who was quickly reinstalled in his palace by Soult's counter-offensive, did not enlist Goya's services on this occasion. His successive comings and goings had done nothing to mar his equanimity. He was no more evil than the next man, just as his younger brother Napoleon was no more unintelligent. It was said, however, that the younger brother felt slightly embarrassed at being junior in years, and that he compensated for his embarrassment by ridiculing all Joseph's opinions on principle. Joseph may well have smiled in later years when he read Talleyrand's summing up of their relationship: 'The two brothers opposed one another in all their activities. It was never possible for them to agree on any course of political action, any financial plan, any military disposition.'

Joseph's pessimistic pronouncements multiplied, both in private conversation and in his official reports. 'I am a puppet responsible for the evil which he can neither foresee nor prevent... I am disgracing myself here like an idiot, a schemer or a self-seeker...' And again: 'My presence here serves no purpose. I must therefore leave Madrid and Spain before a further prolongation of the spectacle of public misery and its inevitable consequences drives me violently away...' Napoleon did not heed these warnings until he was pondering on his past life in St Helena. 'This unhappy war was my undoing; all the circumstances of my disasters are linked with this fatal knot. It complicated my difficulties, divided my forces and destroyed my morality in Europe...'

While awaiting his downfall, which he knew to be inevitable, Joseph Bonaparte resigned himself to reigning as best he could. His royal brother had decided very

EXECUTION OF A WITCH, *c.* 1810

early on that the army must live off the areas it occupied in order to restrict operational costs. This meant that the only people who exercised any real authority in Spain were the heads of the French military zones and the Spanish guerilla leaders: the colonels of the army of occupation on one side, the Junta of Cadiz on the other, and Joseph in the middle.

Joseph seems to have cherished a genuine admiration for the nation that hated him, which partly explains the attitude of Goya and many of his friends. As far as the meagre resources available to him permitted, the 'intruder king' tried – as he had done during his recent spell on the throne of Naples, but with less success – to ensure that his illusory reign did not leave purely negative traces behind. He took part in religious processions, reinstituted the bullfights banned by Godoy, tried to rationalize the civil administration, put a modernization plan into effect in Madrid, and behaved with compassion during the terrible famine which gripped the country in 1811 and caused five thousand deaths by starvation in Madrid alone. He personally distributed bread baked in his palace and sent anonymous gifts of food and money to paupers who were too proud to beg.

Nevertheless, he was still as devoid of illusions as ever when he allowed Soult to reinstate him in Madrid during the autumn of 1812. Two months later he heard the news of the defeat at the Berezina, and this time he prepared to leave the capital for good. The last French troops left Spanish territory in June 1813, after the battle of Vittoria.

Was this the end of the nightmare? Influenced by the few liberals who had joined it, the Junta of Cadiz had tried from the outset to show that it was not opposed to French-inspired social reform even though it did not wish to see it imposed by foreigners. It established freedom of the press, proclaimed the Rights of Man and drafted a constitution – and this at the instigation of a handful of intellectuals, who had not been very numerous before the war of independence and were even less so now that many of the leading 'afrancesados' had been compelled to leave Spain in King Joseph's baggage trains rather than face trial by special tribunal.

At all events, it was the people alone who had won the war. They were even less interested in the editorial freedom of newspapers which they were unable to read than they were in the Rights of Man or the abstract principles governing the mechanism of a constitutional system. What they wanted was compensation for the injury that had been done them. They had been robbed of their 'rey idolatrado', Ferdinand VII, and they wanted him back. Ferdinand himself was utterly insensible to the wind of liberalism that was blowing in his country. While awaiting the moment when Napoleon would be forced to cut his losses and reinstate him on the throne of Spain, he almost set fire to his allotted residence-in-exile, the Château de Valençay – not as part of an escape plan, but because he and his brother had found some shelves containing books by Voltaire and Rousseau in the library there, and had reduced them to cinders.

PORTRAIT OF THE PAINTER ASCENSIO JULIA, 1814-1819

PORTRAIT OF FERDINAND VII, 1814

No, the struggle was far from over yet, and Goya sensed this more than anyone. The piles of mutilated corpses and the frightful accumulation of hatred and misery did not – or not yet, at least – contain the seeds of any kind of freedom.

When, in March 1814, Napoleon sent Ferdinand VII back to the Spanish frontier under escort (retaining his brother as a hostage), Goya was already planning to paint his customary portrait of the monarch as soon as he had made his triumphal entry into Madrid. However, the paintings on which he was currently engaged were the logical outcome and consummation of the *Disasters* series. Six years after the events depicted, he was producing the two large canvases entitled *The Charge of the Mamelukes* and *The Execution of the Defenders of Madrid*. *The Charge of the Mamelukes* epitomizes the heroism of the common people of Spain in a stunning arabesque. The courage of the attackers hurling themselves at the horses, knives in hand, the wild savagery of the Mamelukes and the elegance of the whirling shapes and colours combine to form a vortex of movement beside which the crowd scenes of Delacroix and the other Romantics look like the work of precocious children.

Of all Goya's evocations of the horrors of war, *The Execution of the Defenders of Madrid* is the most consummate and the most representative. It embodies all the *Disasters* in one. '*The Third of May* and some of the *Disasters* are reminiscent of the great novels of Dostoievsky,' writes André Malraux. 'The two artists are suddenly sundered from mankind by the irremediable

A PORTRAIT OF THE DUKE OF WELLINGTON

(and the House of the Deaf Man would have been a worthy habitation for the Karamazovs...). Dostoievsky's novels were, and continue to be, narratives, but they become an affirmation – obscure and urgent like the language of every modern prophet. What is a prophet if not a man who addresses himself to others in order to open their eyes, to wrest them from the world of appearances and give them the world of Truth? And truth to

SELF-PORTRAIT, *c.* 1816

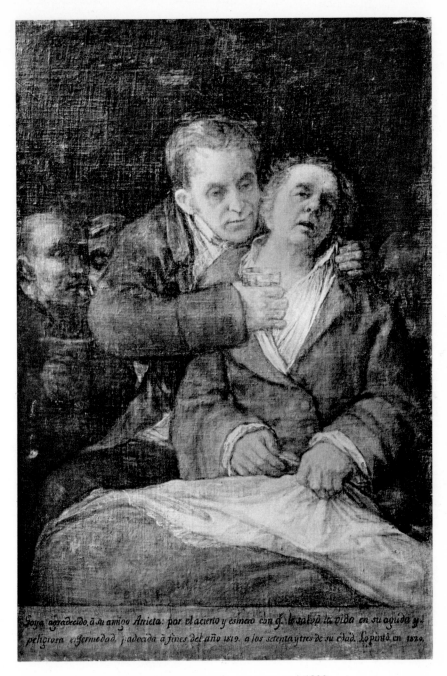

Goya agradecido, á su amigo Arrieta: por el acierto y esmero con q.^e le salvó la vida en su aguda y
peligrosa enfermedad, padecida á fines del año 1819, a los setenta y tres de su edad. Lo pintó en 1820.

SELF-PORTRAIT WITH DR ARRIETA, 1820

a painter is no more a doctrine than it is to a musician: these are paintings which render the world first vulnerable and then illusory. Study madmen to your heart's content, having done so, look in the mirror! Study Goya's art, but, having done so, watch how the world of man totters and reels...'

Look at the swarthy little man who kneels there with arms spread wide, literally crucified in space. Like a human torch, he dominates all the picture's lights and shades. He illuminates the hillock behind him, the arm of the foremost of his faceless executioners, the bodies of those who have already fallen and the features of those who are waiting their turn to die. His eyes, two black holes focused on the muzzles of the firing-squad, convey – even more than fear – a panic horror at the inexorable incomprehensibility of fate; and around this isolated and anonymous human flame reigns the sort of darkness that shrouded the entire world because of one man's sacrifice on a hill called Golgotha.

Some people have inferred that Goya painted this canvas just before Ferdinand VII's return because he wanted to 'atone' for his equivocal attitude during the war of liberation. Apart from the fact that the picture could never have been conceived if Goya had not already drawn, etched or painted two or three hundred works in an identical vein during the four or five preceding years, no form of atonement – if atonement it was – could have carried greater conviction.

A new official career (1814-1819)

When the time came for Ferdinand's return, Goya, now seventy, applied himself diligently to his duties as an official painter – all the more diligently because he had just been acquitted by a tribunal before which he had had to attest solemnly that he had only painted King Joseph's portrait from an engraving and had never actually worn the 'aubergine' which the French had awarded him. His acquittal, however justified, was due less to his reasoned defence than to his immense reputation as a painter, which had made him a source of national pride.

'In our absence you deserved exile – even the garotte, but you are a great artist and we pardon you.' These words, attributed to Ferdinand VII (who was never one to jib at breaking his word), convey some idea of the precarious nature of Goya's semi-rehabilitation and of

BULLFIGHTS: 'THE BRAVE RENDON WOUNDS THE BULL WITH HIS PIKE;
IN SO DOING, HE MEETS HIS DEATH IN THE BULLRING AT MADRID'

BULLFIGHTS: 'HOW THE FAMOUS MARTINCHO PLANTS HIS BANDERILLAS'

BULLFIGHTS: 'THE AGILITY AND DARING OF JUANITO APIÑAÑI
IN THE BULLRING AT MADRID'

the dangers which were bound to beset him if he re-emerged as official painter to the new regime. He promptly started work on a portrait of Ferdinand in coronation robes, followed by another showing him in the uniform of Captain-General. They were portraits in the traditional manner, but portraits in which Goya stinted neither his talent nor his habitual lack of indulgence towards his subject. Few faces could inspire greater misgiving. It is almost impossible to pin down Ferdinand's deformities. Despite his flattering attire he looks uniformly misshapen, in mind as well as body. Scrutinizing the stubborn brow, the cruelty and obscenity in the eyes he inherited from his mother, the slack, contemptuous mouth, the flabby and voluminous chin, one is irresistibly reminded of the perverse and sullen child he must once have been. One can picture him pulling the legs off insects in the gardens of the royal palace, pricking little girls with a pin and then putting his tongue out at them, stealing silver-plate to get the servants into trouble.

It is easier to admire Goya's intimate portraits, with their exemplary and wholly 'modern' freedom of manner, than his official portraits, which are conventional in presentation and more classical in execution. It would, however, be wrong to admire them more. His best official portraits – the ones on which he lavished thought and for which he made preliminary studies – are quite as stimulating as the others, if not more so. As soon as we forget that his sitters are garbed in their Sunday best, we see that they attain a psychological dimension of unsurpassed and probably unsurpassable intensity. The ceremonial occasion on which they have been 'captured' depends only superficially on external circumstances. In reality, it is always situated neatly at the heart of the ideal psychological moment, the moment when, in the unity of time and place, character and personal destiny become fused.

In the same year as he painted Ferdinand VII in the uniform of Captain-General (1815), Goya undertook a portrait of the Duke of San Carlos. Clad in ceremonial dress, the Grand Master of the King's Household strikes one as a man of breeding, self-assured but not unduly conceited, moderately intelligent but not brilliant. If the

King, who professed to be his friend, had been at all receptive to beneficial influences, the Duke of San Carlos would doubtless have played a more important role in the history of the period.

Decorative rather than psychologically illuminating, Goya's large equestrian portrait of General Palafox, painted when the Aragonese resistance hero made his triumphal entry into Madrid, became the object of some rather sordid haggling. Goya was anxious for Palafox to have the picture, but only at a price. He had used materials of good quality, at a time when, he wrote,

TAUROMACHY

'generally speaking, pigments are scarce and oils adultera-ted'.   Palafox was equally anxious to acquire the painting, but not for a fee.   Matters remained there until after Goya's death, when Javier made a renewed effort to sell the portrait to Palafox, whose attitude seems to have been that, all things considered, the price of blood was on a par with that of oil paint.

THE JUNTA OF THE PHILIPPINES (DETAIL), *c.* 1818

BULLFIGHT, 1814

All we know of Goya's approach to business matters indicates with near certainty that he would never have indulged in this haggling if, as some have suggested, he had had to call upon Palafox to testify in his favour before the Tribunal of Rehabilitations. This was more than mere rapacity on Goya's part; it was disillusionment transmuted into aggressive ill-nature. Six years earlier, after Joseph Bonaparte's first and provisional departure, he had painted a portrait of Ferdinand VII free of charge to help celebrate his symbolic restoration. Since then

TAUROMACHY

his enthusiasm had evaporated. After all, Murat's massacre of the Madrileños whom he had just immortalized on canvas had been publicly and spontaneously acclaimed by members of the same Spanish royal family whose supporters now reproached him for having cherished pro-French sympathies. What was more, Ferdinand's first actions on regaining Spanish soil had been to dissolve the Cortés (parliament), tear up the Constitution with scorn and decree the death penalty for those who advocated its principles, restore the Courts of Inquisition and incarcerate King Joseph's *afrancesados* and liberal supporters of the Supreme Junta in the same gaols. And why not? The humble heroes who had hurled themselves bare-handed at Murat's Mamelukes were the same who now cried: 'Death to the liberals! Death to the Constitution! Long live King Ferdinand, the Fatherland and the Nation!' We are also told – a circumstance unique in history and only conceivable in Spain – that they unhitched the horses of the royal carriage and took their place at the shafts with cries of 'Long live fetters!'

Although the consequences of a peace can sometimes be worse than the havoc wrought by war, Goya refused to abandon hope entirely. Being a good Spaniard, he remembered that, whatever social upheavals might rend his country, there was still the bullfight. In 1815 he started on the preliminary drawings for his series of etchings entitled *Bullfights,* designed to illustrate a treatise on the history of Spanish bullfighting by the father of his friend Moratin.

Hieratic violence, ritualized fantasy, the balletic trial of strength between man and beast, the omnipresent odour of horned and untamed death – all the emotional foundations on which the art of tauromachy is based can be found in Goya's episodic battle between light and shade. The conception of the *Bullfights* series occupies a special place in the artist's engravings as a whole. While the *Caprices, Disasters* and *Proverbs* hang together naturally, and their themes recur and are developed at the whim of an inventive mind (e.g. the old man with the stick: 'Still learning'; the shrouded bogey-man of childhood which grows until it becomes the phantom of adult fear: *Colossus,* or *Panic,* etc.), *Bullfights* aims to be a work in its own right. It has an elegance and fierce perfection all

THE WATER-CARRIER, *c.* 1817

its own. In a sense, therefore, the legend that Goya had at one time been a torero (he smiled when questioned on the subject but never replied) is justified. For a certain length of time, Goya neither drew nor painted: he fought bulls in the arena of his mind.

Of the portraits which he still undertook in large numbers between 1814 and 1819, the two which merit special notice are portraits of professional associates: Ascensio Julia, depicted with his arm in a sling at the foot of some scaffolding from which he had fallen – Julia, who lived in Goya's shadow for so long that he could never break free of his old friend's style; and Raphael Estève, who engraved reproductions of Goya's pictures and helped to teach him the techniques of engraving.

Goya could not, of course, dispense with assistants, particularly where large official 'set pieces' were concerned. Discounting Julia and Estève, however, very little is known of his pupil-collaborators. Two names which may be quoted are those of Gil Ranz and Antonio de Brugada, the latter being one of the few intimates capable of soothing Goya's tantrums towards the end of his life in Bordeaux. As for Eugenio Lucas, Goya's faithful and at times extremely skilful imitator, he was not born until 1824, four years before the master's death.

Numerous other portraits of clients or friends came into being at this period, for example those of Don Manuel Garcia de la Prada, of the musician Quijano, of Manuel Garcia, father of La Malibran, of the Duchess of Abrantes, of Don Ignacio Omulzyan and of Don Francisco de Borja, son of the Duchess of Osuna. It was

almost like a return to the far-off days when Goya was forty and high society was falling over itself for the privilege of owning a portrait signed by him.

But the restored monarchy was tightening its hold once more, and Goya felt increasingly constricted. In 1818, after his new career as an official painter had lasted three or four years, he set the seal on it with a majestically unusual work (bought at Madrid in 1881 for thirty-five thousand *reales* by the French painter Briguiboul and preserved in Castres Museum). In this picture, *The Junta of the Philippines,* the almost invisible figure of Ferdinand VII presides over the scene from a central point in the extreme background of the picture, while

218

PROVERBS: 'STRANGE FOLLY', 1814-1819

PROVERBS: 'MATRIMONIAL FOLLY', 1814-1819

the members of the Junta, ranged on either side in unceremonious poses, are separated by a ground painted *au jus* with the mysterious ease and fluidity of a late Manet. This void of grey and rose seems to have been the real subject of the piece.

Goya's career as a society painter had also come to an end. After producing his portrait of the Duchess of Osuna's son he seems to have decided that, at the age of seventy-three, a celebrated painter had the right to refuse further orders and only paint faces for his own pleasure. The great adventure of the Quinta del Sordo was about to begin.

MAJAS WALKING, 1814-1818

The Quinta del Sordo

On 27 February 1819, Goya bought an isolated country house on the far bank of the Manzanares, not far from Madrid. His neighbours soon christened it the Quinta (or Casa) del Sordo – 'Deaf Man's House'.

The months that followed his decision to give up working to order and the first few months after his installation in his new abode were marked by feverish activity. A self-portrait probably executed *c*. 1815 shows the artist looking almost younger than he did in self-portraits of twenty or thirty years before. His features are less drawn, his expression less restless, his eyes softer. At seventy plus, his appearance was that of a forty- or fifty-year-old man in the prime of life.

He was apprehensive, however, not only for his own safety and that of his possessions, but because he sensed the approach of another grave illness. The illness struck him down in due course, but his tough constitution enabled him to survive it, as we can see from the picture (extant only in copies) showing him supported in the arms of his doctor. The inscription at its foot reads: 'Goya, in gratitude to his friend Arrieta for the skill and care which saved his life during the acute and dangerous illness which he suffered at the end of the year 1819, at the age of seventy-three. Painted in 1820.'

The period preceding this illness was not wholly devoted to preparing the plates for *Bullfights*. It was almost as though Goya wanted to send out a final message embodying all his imaginative gifts, all the motives for self-expression, which had inspired him since he first set off down the royal road of 'fantasy and invention'. Ever since the restoration of 1814 he had been drawing other 'disasters' – sentencings, imprisonments, public recantations and the disastrous consequences of the triumph of stupidity in general.

These drawings, which were a stylistic continuation of the *Caprices,* the *Disasters* and his other feats of graphic observation, soon culminated in the first sketches of the *Disparates,* a group of twenty-two etchings of which eighteen were published by the Academy of San Fernando in 1864 under the title of *Proverbs,* now generally accepted as the English designation. It may be added that Goya did not select their original title at random, but intended it to suggest a spiritual affiliation. '*El Disparate*', a purely Spanish word popularly used to denote something foolish, insane or fantastic, was the contemporary sobriquet of Hieronymus Bosch, perhaps the greatest master of fantasy who ever lived.

OLD WOMEN LOOKING IN A MIRROR, 1817-1819

SATURN DEVOURING ONE OF HIS CHILDREN, 1819-1823

Robert Delevoy is right to emphasize that this was 'a new descent into the inferno, a new return to the teratology of the monsters, mysterious apparitions and proverbs comprising the popular lore of the ages'. Engraved with an even firmer and less 'anecdotal' touch than the *Caprices,* the *Proverbs* resemble one of those last wills which some testators like to have read aloud to their heirs after their death. They seem to take to task those whose principles, fads or functions in the social order had, throughout his lifetime, weighed heavily on a man who had at last broken free of them by 'flying off' to another world where he hoped never to hear tell of them again.

Launched across metaphysical voids accessible to them alone, the 'flying men' of the *Proverbs* are soaring away from a kingdom ruled by the blind and uncontrollable stupidity which Goya detested so much and which he expressed in one etching after another.

In painting, *The Old Women, Old Women and Young Women* and *Celestina* exploit another source of inspiration, expressing with paroxysmal intensity a bitterness which is all the more aggressive because it implies inconsolable disappointment at the fact that physical and moral ugliness is part of man's heritage. The figures in the almost contemporaneous *Manolas on the Balcony* (Groult Collection) have undergone a transfiguration. They still lean on the same balustrade, looking down at the beholder with abstracted expressions on their faces, which are slightly more impasted, but their piquant commonness has a less studied and more comforting quality.

Then, again, there was religious inspiration, awakened by the imminence of death. Also dating from this period are *The Communion of San José de Calasanz* and *The Prayer in the Garden of Olives,* two pictures which have already been mentioned in connection with the frescos of San Antonio de la Florida, painted twenty-two years earlier. Their technical perfection merits comparison with the best of Rembrandt, and they are – to reiterate – among the most exalted pictorial expressions of mysticism in Catholic Christendom.

Then, again – for Goya was eternally experimenting – these various sources of inspiration were joined in 1819 by yet another medium of expression. Three years after it had conquered the ateliers of Paris in 1816, he introduced Spain to lithography, invented by Senefelder at Leipzig in 1796.

Unwitting friends were surprised to see him prop a stone slab on his easel instead of a canvas and set to work on it with pencils, which he handled like brushes and with the same rapidity. He brushed in his masses without retouching, sometimes rubbing or scratching the surface of the grey-tinted stone, sometimes using a razor to pick faces or forms out of the grey ground, stroke by stroke. Nothing could have accorded better with Goya's love of spontaneity than a process whose simplicity and immediacy enabled him to conjure with the interplay of light and shade. Goya's first known lithograph depicts an old woman spinning. It originated in February 1819, the month in which he moved to his country retreat.

THE COLOSSUS, OR PANIC, *c.* 1815

Convinced that the Quinta del Sordo was to be his last abode on earth, Goya adorned its walls with something even better than a last will and testament: the famous *pinturas negras* or 'black paintings', pictorial monologues devised for the benefit of himself alone. He had passed the stage of wanting to please or shock. No public stood between him and his art. Having undergone all the usual trials – the easy temptations born of talent and success, the pressures of misfortune and prosperity – he was now confronted by the greatest trial of all, the trial of strength between himself and his *raison d'être,* which was painting.

Two females held sway over the Quinta del Sordo: Doña Leocadia, the half-mistress, half-housekeeper who had recently entered Goya's life, and her daughter Rosarito. Doña Leocadia, née Zorilla, was a distant cousin of the painter who had fallen on hard times. Brusque, touchy, shrewish and quick-tempered, her character was not unlike Goya's own. Her real name was Frau Weiss, and she had been married to a Bavarian whose family had settled in Spain for commercial reasons but who had disappeared one day, leaving her with a son, Guillermo, and a daughter, Maria del Rosario.

Goya, who adored children, was absolutely besotted with Rosarito. The deaf and irascible old man would put up with anything, provided he could watch her trotting through his garden or stroll with her along the shady avenues near his home. Rosarito could twist him round her little finger – even to the extent of making him put up with the vagaries of the shrewish Leocadia –

THE FATES, 1819-1823

but the house whose walls were soon to be populated
by gloomy and grimacing phantoms must have been
a strange setting for a childhood.

'Experts have taken long enough to discover the sub-
terranean passages that lead from our Mardi-Gras to the
world of the dead. But, if Goya did not know the
ramifications of the supernatural, he did sense its relation-

THE PILGRIMAGE OF SAN ISIDRO, 1819-1823

TWO WOMEN LAUGHING, 1819-1823

ships.   Just as other people have emerged from appalling illnesses as mediums, he came back from his own wreathed in an other-wordly fog which disturbed and intrigued rather than terrified him, but which called in question the world from which he had withdrawn.   His demons are as familiar to him as trained beasts are to the buffoons who put them through their paces; but he knows that, although they are only so to him, they can enthral everyone...'

To this quotation from André Malraux's comments on the *Caprices,* works engraved thirty years earlier in which 'the frontier between the face and what is substituted for it is no longer discernible', might be added another, this time from Baudelaire: 'There is, in profoundly individual works (of art), something resembling those recurrent dreams which regularly haunt our sleep...' To recognize this is to begin to grasp the importance of the phenomenon – particularly unique in the history of painting – represented by the 'black Goyas' of the Quinta del Sordo.

The visitor was surrounded by huge rectangular compositions (both of horizontal and vertical format) painted directly in oils on the walls of the large ground-floor room which was used as a dining-room. Beside the entrance, a fleshy but still youthful-looking *maja* leant dreamily on a rock surmounted by a balustrade.   Opposite her, a Judith with a mask-like countenance brandished her reeking sword. Beside her an enormous Saturn with starting eyes devoured a small human body. To the right of the door a bearded old man (the same whom

Goya drew and engraved many times above the legend 'Still learning') leaned painfully on a large stick while a frightful creature with a low forehead mouthed unheard words in his ear. Above the door, a witch with a hooked nose and a malevolent smile cooked something in a pot, surrounded by vaguely human shapes, one of which had a death's head.

Every inch of free space was covered. On one of the walls a motley procession of tattered, drunken figures five yards long straggled along a rocky mountain pad: this was the *Romeria de San Isidro,* a picaresque rejoinder to the *Procession of San Isidro,* which could be seen on another wall. The satanic *Witches' Sabbath* was also there, separated by a million miles from the comparatively restrained and decorative *Witches' Sabbath* which Goya painted for the Duchess of Osuna's reception rooms. Seated on his hind-quarters and seen in profile, the dark, shaggy beast was indoctrinating a circle of squatting crones whose expressions and grimaces ran the gamut of surliness, misery, suspicion and criminality.

Visitors privileged to enter the painter's study were greeted by the nightmare vision of a gap-toothed, laughing woman. Beside her, a group of wretched-looking creatures clustered round a 'reader' whose eyes were cast down, if not sightless. Elsewhere, two men armed with clubs and knee-deep in mud fought to the death according to Aragonese custom. More vivid in colouring but stranger still was the couple floating in the sky near an enormous cliff surmounted by a citadel of the kind which had always haunted Goya. Finally, there was the

disturbing trio of Fates and a dog's head, the only figurative element visible on a vertical panel dominated by a vast and amorphous torrent of burnt sienna.

This dog's head merits particular attention in that, of all the Goyas on display in the Prado since the end of the Second World War, it has proved the biggest draw to a certain category of visitors. Youthful foreigners whose over-casual style of dress marks them as would-be painters and sculptors of the *avant-garde* flock in every day to pay homage to it. The dog, whose thin muzzle scarcely projects above the sand which almost obscures it, would, if it could hear at all, overhear some strange comments – comments uttered in a Babylonian assortment

of tongues but in which the same words nearly always recur: 'Zen painting... non-figurative... authentically and uniquely pictorial... metaphysics of space... abstractionism... non-being...'

Goya, who was too classical (except in his engravings) for the Romantics, too romantic for the Impressionists and too realistic for the Cubists, has suddenly become, by virtue of a single painting and a few sepia sketches which feature vague masses of light and shade, a sort of ancestor of the 'non-figurative' painters of today.

Are our 'non-figurative' artists really descendants of Goya? It would take too long and involve too much of a digression to discuss the question here, but it does appear that, far from being an unfinished picture as some have believed, the panel corresponds to a deliberate intention on the artist's part. Having distorted circumstantial appearances so as to endow them with transcendental significance, Goya went on to attack form itself. He aim was to exorcize and anaesthetize form as well, either by abolishing the need for it or, if not, by reducing it to its essential mechanisms.

This was an extension of the graphic plane of the general anathema constituted by the bulk of the 'black paintings' of the Quinta del Sordo, an anathema directed not only at human folly – war, for example – but at humanity itself, which Goya accused of functioning as an eternal instrument of destructive stupidity.

Realizing that all his warnings and predictions had been fruitless, Goya no longer lent shape to his fears and revulsions in order to put his fellow-men on their guard; he did so in order to 'fix' them for ever so that they could no longer assail him personally. He captured his demons and monsters and pinned them to the walls of what he believed to be his last home. He painted them to reassure himself that he had dominated them, and he kept his eye on them to reassure himself that they could never stir again without his approval. Having decorated the tomb of his imagination, he lived in it and waited.

The traditional name for these murals, 'black paintings', probably derives from the fact that many people have sensed, if not understood, the dramatically sombre nature of their motivation. It is not an apt description. In general, Goya applied his paints on a ground of burnt sienna and seville, but any monochrome impression created by this vanishes on closer inspection. In fact, Goya never showed greater skill in utilizing all his colours, in arranging and diffusing them so that they did exactly what he expected of them, which was to sustain and activate the tonal values of his painting. As for his genuine 'black paintings', it is difficult to view them properly in their ground-floor room in the Prado. They would become more intelligible – more readily 'legible' – if they were housed in a building where they could be seen as Goya once arranged them in his own home.

This would set the seal on the work of Baron d'Erlanger, the French banker and art-lover who saved the Black Paintings for posterity by buying the Quinta del Sordo in 1873 and having the murals mounted on canvas. He then had them transported to Paris with the intention of presenting them to the Louvre, but first exhibited them at the Exposition Universelle of 1878. Drugged with Impressionism, the enlightened art-lovers and eminent critics of the day shared the general public's view that they were merely an expression of tumultuous, clumsy and monotonous ugliness. Baron d'Erlanger was so appalled by their incomprehension that he took his pictures back to Madrid and offered them to the Prado.

Thus, although Spain owed France the horrors of the Peninsular War, she was indebted to a Frenchman for preserving the works of art without which we might not be tempted to compare Goya's genius with that of Shakespeare or Dostoievsky.

'Long live fetters!'

A new wind of freedom was blowing from Cadiz. On 1 January 1820, supported by ill-paid soldiers who were about to embark for America, where the façade of the old Spanish empire was collapsing in ruins, liberal nationalists reaffirmed the principle of constitutional monarchy which had been adopted ten years earlier by the anti-Bonapartist Junta.

Within days, the movement had swept the country. Ferdinand VII beat a strategic retreat and set about regaining control by dint of background manœuvres. On a fine April morning in the same year, Don Francisco Goya's barouche left the Quinta del Sordo and headed for Madrid. The old painter had emerged from solitude for one day in answer to a summons from the Academy, where members were gathered in solemn session to swear allegiance to the Constitution. The almost optimistic

PORTRAIT OF MARIANO GOYA (THE ARTIST'S GRANDSON), 1817

drawing of Justice driving away bats with a whip ('Divine Reason spares none of them') undoubtedly dates from this period.

This, however, was to be the last Academy meeting which Goya ever attended. The situation deteriorated rapidly and became increasingly confused. Administrative chaos was accompanied by latent civil war, the reappearance of 'grand companies' in the countryside, assassinations, overflowing prisons and more general misery and suffering than before. Summer 1822 saw the highroads of Spain roamed by bands of royalists calling themselves the Army of the Faith. Ferdinand VII set up a 'Regency for the duration of the King's captivity' – which he disowned for form's sake – and sent emissaries to Paris to persuade Louis XVIII that Spain was experiencing a recrudescence of the French Revolution.

Alarmed, Louis XVIII officially announced in his speech from the throne of January 1823 that France intended to intervene: 'A hundred thousand Frenchmen are ready to march, calling upon the God of Saint Louis, to preserve the throne of Spain for a grandson of Henry IV.' Eight months later, the Duke of Angoulème and his hundred thousand Frenchmen concluded a triumphal military promenade by investing Cadiz on the night of 30-31 August 1823. French officers who had taken part in the 1808 campaign were astonished to find that their bitter enemies of yore – e.g. the victor of Baylen – welcomed them with open arms.

From Cadiz, where he had been 'kept under surveillance', the Duke of Angoulème's troops conveyed

Ferdinand VII back to Madrid. Their mission had been not only to give him back his throne but to obtain from him, in exchange for services rendered, an undertaking to restore domestic order, abandon his baneful plans for reprisals and renounce an absolute monarchy whose very existence threatened to provoke renewed disturbances. Nothing, however, could prevent Ferdinand from wreaking vengeance now that he had regained power – a power which he intended to retain for himself alone.

Having exhausted all the arts of persuasion, the Duke of Angoulême lost patience: 'It is with regret that I find myself obliged to submit to Your Majesty that all France's efforts to liberate Your Majesty will be rendered futile if Your Majesty continues to maintain the pernicious system of government which led to the misfortunes of 1820. In the two weeks since Your Majesty regained authority, nothing is yet known of Your Majesty but arrests and arbitrary decrees. Thus, anxiety, terror and discontent are beginning to spread everywhere.' Hundreds of lives and vast sums of money had been squandered in vain. An army of one hundred thousand men had marched to no avail. The French decided that the best policy was to cut their losses and go home. 'There is nothing good to be accomplished here,' the Duke of Angoulême wrote to Louis XVIII. 'This country will be tearing itself apart for many years to come.'

The Duke departed, his ears still ringing with the shouts of the crowd below Ferdinand's balcony: 'Long live the King! Long live absolute monarchy! Long live fetters!'

Deaf though he was, Goya heard this monstrous cry in his country retreat. He was under no illusions. This time, all hope of speedy deliverance from the yoke of absolutism had gone, and he was seventy-seven years old. On 17 September 1823, less than three weeks after Ferdinand's liberation by the French at Cadiz, he took the initial precaution of making over the Quinta del Sordo to his grandson Mariano, so that the house which he had decorated for himself could not be confiscated. It was clear that the King was not going to make any exceptions in the case of suspects, even where a celebrated artist like Don Francisco Goya was concerned. Doña Leocadia, whose son Guillermo had compromised himself by joining the constitutional militia, fled to Bordeaux, the rallying-point of the victims of the restoration, taking little Rosarito with her. All Goya's friends were going into exile one by one, and many of them begged him to follow their example. For an old man who had never set foot outside his own country except when visiting Italy more than fifty years before, it was a hard decision to take.

As a final gesture of appeasement he painted a society portrait of Don Ramón Satur, Alcalde of the Court and nephew of Don José Duaso y Latro, the eccentric but erudite canon who pioneered mountain-climbing in Spain. Don José's resolutely anti-liberal ideas had earned him the post of censor to the Madrid press, but he gladly gave liberals his personal protection. What was more, he was an Aragonese like Goya.

Goya took refuge in Duaso's house for several months while the so-called White Terror which raged throughout

PORTRAIT OF DON FRANCISCO DEL MAZO, *c.* 1820

Spain was at its height.   He was now seventy-eight, and the course of events had so upset him that he found it impossible to complete a 'bread-and-butter' portrait of his host and protector, even at the fourth attempt.

The old painter sank into a kind of torpor, just as he had done after the Duchess of Alba's death – just as he had done throughout his long career whenever he was deeply distressed or gravely disappointed.

Elie Faure, whose natural generosity prompts him, authoritatively and unreservedly, to number Goya among the heroes of research into the absolute, disregards such attacks of weakness.   Nevertheless, Goya's months in retreat at Canon Duaso's house during the long winter of 1823-4 were not, as Faure has suggested, dominated by dreams of 'riddling the Inquisition with arrows, boxing the Bourbons' ears and slaughtering the French'. What was the point of continuing to paint, of straining his eyesight – which had been deteriorating for some time – in order to enrich the storehouse of his imagination, when there was a risk that everything he had created might be destroyed at any moment and in the worst conceivable way.

The death which haunted him was not that of an old man whose cup was overflowing with the joy to which his age entitled him, but that of an old painter, outlawed and perhaps even imprisoned, who would be asked to turn his back on a whole career without any hope of resuming it again.   Were the monsters of evil and stupidity which had always menaced him and made him tremble destined to have the final word?

He had tried to exorcize them in the *Caprices, Disasters* and *Proverbs*. He had even anathematized them by pinning them to the walls of the Quinta del Sordo. But, though they were prisoners in the guise which he had imposed on them, there was no evidence that other and more potent enchantments could not release them, enabling them to wreak their revenge on the man who had tried to keep them at his mercy – an elderly painter whose sole remaining safeguard was the charity of a member of the very party whose myrmidons were waiting to pounce on him. The next time the door opened noiselessly, it might open to reveal a minion of the Inquisition.

It seemed utterly inconceivable at the beginning of 1824 that any wind of change would ever dispel the gloom that shrouded the Spanish sky. As things were, the situation could only deteriorate. The net was closing about Goya. His only alternative, provided there was still time, was exile.

He hesitated. The word exile frightened him. He wanted to leave the country, but not if it entailed abandoning everything. The crafty peasant in him took steps to ensure that he would be able to emigrate without being exiled, since this would mean forfeiting his title of First Painter to the King and the salary that went with it. At his age he was entitled to be ill, and it was his doctors' duty to prescribe suitable treatment. It turned out that this treatment could only be undertaken properly in France – at the spa of Plombières, to be precise. Matters were clinched on 30 May 1824, when the Grand Majordomo of the Court granted him six months' leave of absence: 'Our Lord the King, yielding to the request of the Court Painter Don Francisco Goya, has been pleased to grant him His Majesty's royal permission to go to take the mineral waters at Plombières, in France, in order to alleviate his rheumatism.'

Armed with his safe-conduct to Plombières, Goya set off for Paris via Bordeaux. It was the first time he had ever crossed the Pyrenees, and he had never felt younger.

A MANOLA, 1819-1823

Apotheosis, metamorphosis and transfiguration

'Goya has arrived, old, deaf, enfeebled, not knowing a word of French and without a servant – and who could need one more than he? – but nevertheless very contented and very eager to see the world.'

Leandro Moratin, who had welcomed his old friend on his way through Bordeaux, felt more than a little worried. Even a young man would have been tired after such a long journey. Not only was Goya an old man, but few of his juniors would have displayed such fierce and intense enthusiasm at the idea of seeing the world. There was no holding him. 'He ate with us for two days, like a young schoolboy,' reported Moratin, who had opened a boarding school in Bordeaux with his friend Manuel Silvela. 'I advised him to come back in September and not to get held up in Paris nor caught by the winter... We shall not know if he survives the journey until later. I should be deeply distressed if any harm came to him.' Goya was heedless of the anxiety he was causing. In a business letter written to his son Javier at this time he remarked that it was well within the bounds of possibility that he would emulate Titian, who was erroneously reputed to have attained the age of ninety-nine. He was enjoying a holiday for the first time in his life.

The only periods of inactivity in his career had been periods when over-activity had laid him low. This time he was indulging, quite alone, in the luxury of 'tourism'. He had forgotten the few words of French which he had learned in the far-off days when he believed the language

STILL-LIFE, *c.* 1820

would guarantee his social reputation, but what did that matter to a deaf man? All good tourists being Englishmen at heart, he entered Paris with his massive head encased in an enormous checked cap!

Painting was the prevailing topic of conversation in the French capital, where the Salon of 1824 had provoked violent controversy. Constable was exhibiting landscapes, Géricault his *Raft of the 'Medusa'* and Delacroix the *Massacre of Chios*. It was a vintage year.

In Paris, however, Spain's most celebrated painter was merely a face in the crowd. The only French colleague to welcome him and steer him through the Parisian jungle was Horace Vernet, a good but minor painter who was distantly related to one of Goya's friends. To a constellation of young artists squabbling over pictorial problems which he himself had solved long ago, the Spanish Court Painter with his grandiose title and his English-style cap clamped firmly on his Aragonese cranium must have looked like an old war-horse from another age. It is highly probable that Vernet took him to see *Massacre of Chios* and *Raft of the 'Medusa'*, but there is no evidence that he was impressed by them.

Goya only brought back one locally inspired work from the French capital, a drawing of some dogs pulling a small cart and inscribed '*Yo lo visto en Paris*'. For the rest, he confined himself to producing portraits of Spaniards – Joaquim Maria Ferrier and his wife, his friends and hosts – and to painting some bulls from memory. With the approach of autumn, Goya, who had never meant to set foot in Plombières anyway, followed Moratin's advice and returned to Bordeaux.

Almost as much Spanish was spoken in the streets of Bordeaux at this period as French, for this was where most of the émigrés had settled down to await the first opportunity to retrace their steps across the Pyrenees. They were a strange assortment, many of them having fought against each other in the course of their tragic and troubled lives. Just as Ferdinand's gaols had indiscriminately housed *afrancesados,* liberal partisans of the Cadiz Junta and all who had incurred royal displeasure for any reason, so a motley collection of customers frequented the chocolate shop which had been opened in the Rue de la Petite Taupe (now the Rue de la Huguerie) by Braulio Poc, a veteran of the siege of Zaragoza. His patrons included supporters of ex-King Joseph, Catholics, anti-clerical freemasons, moderate conservative monarchists, progressive 'constitutionalists' and liberals of every complexion whom the harsh exigencies of exile had forced into coexistence – all the more so because, surrounded by puzzled foreign observers, they were the only people who could thread their way through what the British sociologist Gerald Brenan has christened 'the Spanish labyrinth'. There even existed, among these variegated political outcasts, Spaniards whose passports were in order, and who could, if they were careful, shuttle to and fro between Bordeaux and Madrid. One of these was Goya, whose post as Court Painter carried the same official status under the new regime as it had under its predecessors.

He took good care not to sever relations with the Court. When his six months' leave of absence was up, he requested and was granted another six months – ostensibly to undertake a cure nearer the frontier, at Bagnères, which saw no more of him than Plombières had done.

Shielded by distance from the vagaries of Ferdinand VII and living among friends who respected him, Goya declared himself delighted with the city, the countryside, the climate, the food, and the independence and tranquillity which he now enjoyed. After renting an apartment at 24 Cours de Tourny, he bought a small house (10 Rue de la Croix-Blanche) which Moratin described as 'extremely

SPANISH DIVERSION, 1825

well-appointed, with north and south lights'. He purchased it in the name of Doña Leocadia, who never
failed to astound the worthy Moratin with her 'customary
intrepidity', her stormy and unpredictable lamentations
and her equally unpredictable outbursts of joy. 'Rain
alternates with fair weather,' he noted resignedly. 'I do
not perceive any great harmony between them.' But
there was still Rosarito. Doña Leocadia's daughter was
now about twelve years old, and Goya could walk through
the streets with her, hand in hand, marvelling at what
amused her and being amused by what she marvelled at.

The child's carefree acceptance of exile and her immediate acclimatization to the new environment in which she found herself were both a lesson to Goya and a source of consolation. What overjoyed him most, however, was that Rosarito showed a considerable talent for drawing and painting. (Her career proved to be a short one. Having worked as a copyist at the Prado and been appointed Queen Isabella's drawing mistress, she died of a neglected fever at the age of twenty-six, on a day when Madrid was once again rent by civil strife.)

After a brief but almost fatal illness, Goya, now eighty, went back to work with a will. He had to don several pairs of glasses and, on occasions, use a magnifying glass when tackling a canvas or lithographic plate, but this did not prevent him from escorting Rosarito on her daily visits to the Bordeaux paper merchant who was instructing her in the rudiments of drawing, nor from inspecting the studio of Antoine Lacour, a pupil of David, to whom he had also entrusted the child for instruction. His comment on the canvases displayed there was a grumpy '*No es eso!*' (That's not it!)

To his adoring eyes, Rosarito possessed all talents in abundance. He even considered parting with her and sending her off to study in Paris. 'The amazing child wishes to learn to do miniatures,' he wrote to his friend Ferrier, 'and I wish it as well, for to do at her age what she has done is the most phenomenal thing in the world. She possesses special qualities, as you will see... I should like you to look upon her as if she were my daughter... I shall repay you...' Meanwhile, he had taken up miniatures himself. 'Last winter', he wrote to Ferrier in December 1825, 'I painted on ivory, and I have a collection of nearly forty of these efforts. It is an original type of miniature and one which I have not seen before, because they are done in stipple, and there are things in them which resemble the brushwork of Velazquez and Mengs.' By referring to the painter whom he admired most and the most celebrated painter of his younger days, he hoped to attract custom and make Ferrier his 'impresario'.

As for Ferrier, how could he explain to an elderly painter whose prestige and popularity was second to none in his own country that he was unsaleable beyond its frontiers because, in stock market terminology, he did not possesses an international 'quotation'? Discreetly, he advised Goya to copy or re-issue the *Caprices,* several prints of which were circulating in Parisian studios. These being the only products of his genius known in Paris, the public relations man in Ferrier felt that Goya should make them his point of departure. However, Goya was still painting admirable portraits and had embarked on a whole series of lithographs – the *Bulls of Bordeaux, Love, Jealousy, El Vito* – which demonstrated his complete mastery of the dramatic art of black and white. That he should copy the *Caprices,* whose plates he had presented to the King of Spain a quarter of a century before, struck him as a monstrous suggestion: 'I am certainly not going to copy them', he replied, 'being in possession of new items which should sell to good advantage.' Unhappily, his idea of the commercial value of his products bore no relation to the potentials of the new market for which they were intended.

His prolonged leave of absence having expired, Goya set off for Madrid. King Ferdinand accorded him a benevolent reception and requested a portrait of him from Vincente Lopez, who shared the title of First Painter. Better still, he granted the old man unlimited leave of absence, thus guaranteeing him a salary for the rest of his life. Goya, who had been uneasy when he arrived in Madrid in May 1826, arrived back in Bordeaux on 17 June of the same year with his mind at rest, accompanied by his grandson Mariano. Goya's Bordeaux 'period' is remarkable in that it represents a metamorphosis as well as an apotheosis. On the eve of his death, Goya came within an ace of becoming a typically French painter. Animals from the circus in the Rue des Manèges, beggars, stall-keepers, crowds – he drew them all as fluently as he had drawn the *manolos* and popular festivals of his own country. But the nervous tension was no longer there. Instead, there was a contentment which nullified the ugliness and hatred. The ritual cruelty of the bullfight vanished in a gorgeous impasto of luminous colour. *The Milkmaid of Bordeaux,* a gently authoritative epitome of the unborn Renoir's future work, seems less astonishing when one realizes that it was not an exception in Goya's *œuvre* but the continuation of a style which could only have reached full flower under a French sky, a style already heralded by the peasants in Goya's tapestry cartoons à la Bayeu (but more subtle) or in the Budapest *Water-carrier* of 1917, painted à la Greuze (but with greater passion).

On 3 March 1828, Javier Goya, who had announced his intention of visiting his father, received a latter from him at Barcelona written in a trembling hand: 'My dear Javier, I cannot tell you more, so much happiness has made me ill and I am in bed. God grant you come... then my joy will be complete, adieu. Your father, Francisco.'

The above was accompanied by a few lines from Mariano, the grandson who had inherited the Quinta del Sordo: 'Dear Father, Grandfather has added these four lines to the end of my letter, which proves to you that he is still alive.'

In reality, Goya had just collapsed in his studio, brush in hand. A month before he had survived a stroke which left him partially paralyzed. Did he realize, at the age of eighty-two, that he was destined to die seven years earlier than Titian? During the night of 14-15 March 1828, a fortnight before his eighty-second birthday, he momentarily emerged from his torpor and stared at the hand that had painted so many hundreds of pictures, almost as if he were surprised to see it lying inert. Then he entered his death-throes.

Goya was buried beside his friend Goicoechea, who had died three years earlier, in the Muguiro family's plot in the Carthusian cemetery at Bordeaux. Some pious hand adorned his grave with a small Virgin in white plaster, but this was soon overgrown with moss. His remains lay there neglected for sixty years, until they were exhumed in the presence of the Spanish consul on 16 November 1888. It turned out that his skull had disappeared, possibly stolen by one of the Acalophiles with whom he had been friendly while he was engraving the *Caprices,* and who, besides being 'lovers of ugliness', were noted for their interest in phrenology. His remains were first transferred to San Isidro in 1899, but it was not until the centenary of his death in 1928 that they were removed to San Antonio de la Florida and laid to rest beneath the domed ceiling which he had painted with such restless fervour a hundred and thirty years before.

Great painters do not die, but they sometimes have to undergo a long period of incomprehension and indifference at the beginning of their posthumous careers. It is as though history were repeating itself in a different way. Their posthumous 'youth' is beset by difficulties comparable with those that afflicted them in their early days on earth.

The fact is that a painter's lifetime reputation, like that of a writer or composer, is generally founded on criteria which differ from those that permit his work to survive after his death. Thus, a certain length of time must elapse before we can forget his immediate fame and rediscover a creative personality which his contemporaries would be surprised to find us appreciating for qualities which they themselves discounted altogether. In the case of Goya, who was born in the isolation of Spain and closely linked by his personal destiny to the singular destiny of his country, the position was even more complicated. The world not only had to accustom itself to his particular form of genius. It had, in addition, to penetrate the rugged mountain barrier that divides Spain from the rest of Europe.

Furthermore, as I have already indicated, Goya was known for several decades only by his etchings, notably the *Caprices,* a work which may be regarded as preliminary to his artistic development because it dates from the period when he was only just beginning to blaze a trail of his own. The public and, more especially, the public in Paris, which was already assuming the status of a world art centre, was not called upon to judge Goya's other etchings until long after his death *(Bullfights* in 1855, *Proverbs* in 1864 and *Disasters* in 1870).

It is true that Goya's son sold several of his paintings abroad in 1834, but almost all of them slumbered on undisturbed in the salons – or attics – of their original purchasers. This, of course, was one of the reasons why people did not really begin to form an idea of Goya's whole *œuvre* until the end of the nineteenth century, but it was not the only reason nor even, perhaps, the most important.

It is odd that of all the nineteenth-century artists who longed for a new renaissance and strove to extricate themselves from the paralyzing embrace of neo-Classicism by every possible means – Romanticism included – none was prompted to suspect the real importance of Goya's work. The little that was known of him should have been enough to put alert minds on his track, but it was not enough even for Baudelaire, perhaps the most intuitive and intelligent art critic of all time. Naturally, Baudelaire could not remain indifferent to the 'sombre and fantastic' genius of Goya, but these two adjectives define the extent of the genius with which he was prepared to credit him. 'He reminds me of Rembrandt and Watteau, Hogarth and Callor. He is a sad, sceptical Cervantes-turned-Voltairian. The light of Velazquez and the colour of Greco died with him.'

Louis Viardot, the first serious translator of Don Quixote into French, seems to have been on the point of discovering Goya. Returning from one of his trips to Spain in 1834, he tried to convince friends from various Romanticist coteries that the author of the *Caprices* was a great painter as well as an engraver – that he was *'la seule individualité puissante de l'Espagne d'aujour-d'hui'*. However, he qualified this assertion by defining Goya's unique talent as 'owing nothing to the past and incapable of giving anything to the future'.

Victor Hugo was among those whose knowledge of Goya was limited to his early etchings, which he much admired. It has even been said that they played a decisive part in the development of his own graphic art, but the affinities between Hugo's paintings, drawings and wash-drawings – admirable though they are – and the *Caprices,* for example, are of the vaguest. If one must associate Hugo's drawings with a tradition, the German or English Romantics seem far more likely candidates than Goya, who, as has been evident throughout this account, remained as impervious to Romanticism as he did to any other aesthetic trend.

We have already had occasion to quote some passages from Hugo's account of his journey through strife-torn

THE MILKMAID OF BORDEAUX, 1826-1828

Spain at the age of nine, passages which might serve as a footnote to Goya's unforgettable visions of horror. It is significant, however, that Hugo himself never noted any affinity between them until 1870, when he was thumbing through an edition of the *Disasters* for the first time, almost at the end of his life. Even then, he seems to have been insensible to the etchings' bold composition and to the chiaroscuro technique which had, on his own admission, influenced him so greatly. 'Beautiful and hideous' was his only comment. In fact, like Baudelaire and the bulk of his contemporaries, Hugo regarded Goya as no more than a fabricator of 'beautiful hideosities' – a sort of exotic Daumier.

This view was also shared by Delacroix. It may be noted in passing that the legend according to which Delacroix introduced Hugo to Goya seems unlikely in view of the fact that the former, a reserved, intelligent, sensitive person, had an undisguised aversion to the extravagant and boisterous vitality of the latter.

The Romantics could not and would not see anything but the 'charged' side of Goya's work. They appreciated his picturesque, not his pictorial world, which meant that their approach to the question was essentially literary. Manet was the first major painter to take a painter's interest in Goya, though caution is still indicated when examining their affinity.

The relationship between many of Manet's canvases (*The Balcony, Woman with a Fan, Lola de Valence,* etc.) and paintings of similar subjects by Goya is evident – too evident, in fact. They are brilliant replicas, but replicas for all that – not paintings sustained by an experiment which they are pursuing on their own behalf. Goya may be said to have developed Velazquez and Rembrandt, but Manet was no developer of Goya. He found him a source of inspiration, but that was all. Although he was the first to realize that Goya's greatness lay in the impassioned accuracy of his evocations of atmosphere far more than in his choice of subjects, Manet, an essentially French painter, produced variations on 'Goyesque' themes. This did not make his painting any more Goyesque than it did that of the Impressionists who were soon to regard him as their prophet.

The Romantics considered Goya to be a visionary. The Impressionists regarded him as a sordid realist. The blend of indifference and disgust with which leading connoisseurs of the period greeted the Quinta del Sordo paintings when they were displayed at the 1878 Exhibition, during the hey-day of Impressionism, is proof enough of this. Besides, no one had been unduly indignant ten years earlier, in 1868, when a hack critic named Lachaise had greeted the Louvre's acquisition of Goya's admirable (and admirably classical!) portrait of Guillemardet in the following terms: 'Our museum has just received a portrait by Goya, whom lovers of false realism praise to the skies. Its flashy colouring, shaky modelling and undistinguished pose are hardly such as to prompt us to retract the views which we have already expressed on this artist's type of talent. It is merely an attempt at Velazquez, nothing more, and his attempts fall far short of compositions by Boilly, Vernet, Bosio, etc.'

How many people care about Boilly, Vernet or Bosio today? The fact is that Romantic tumult was as inconsistent with grandiose Goyesque orchestrations as the delicate chamber music of Impressionism.

Even today, Goya is too often appreciated only in part. Some people like to see him as a sort of painter-adventurer (which he was anything but) and others as a politically committed artist (which he was without meaning to be); others, again, praise the engraver and chide the portraitist, and the majority do not know which category to put him in. There's the rub, and there, too, is where Goya's baffling greatness lies.

There are dozens of Goyas, but, whether we like it or not, they all add up to one. Here, in brief, are a few of them: a typical eighteenth-century painter, as witness *The Meadow of San Isidro,* his best tapestry cartoons and his large-scale formal portraits; a typical nineteenth-century painter (from the *Charge of the Mamelukes* to the *Milkmaid of Bordeaux,* the seeds of every phase in nineteenth-century painting, from Géricault to Renoir via Turner and Ensor, are already contained in his work); a perfectly conventional official portraitist; a 'psychological' portraitist of unrivalled perception; a historical painter; a religious painter in the commercial and decorative sense; an inspired religious painter, as witness the Chapel of San Antonio and the *Communion of San José;* an anti-clerical and polemical genre painter; a landscape painter who was uncommonly receptive to the beauties of Nature; an engraver who has been justly compared with Rembrandt and, more debatably, with

Callot and Daumier; a savagely realistic Expressionist, as witness *The Old Women;* an imaginative Expressionist, as witness the *Proverbs;* a tender and affectionate child-portraitist; a moralist, sometimes a trifle naive, sometimes brilliantly concise, as witness the commentaries to his etchings; a sensualist, as witness the two *Majas;* a lover of the people, as witness the townsfolk and peasants who throng his work as a whole; a society painter who was prepared to accept any commission that came his way; a man who, despite his rapacity, was capable of painting for his own pleasure and out of an apparent sense of duty to himself, as witness the murals from the Quinta del Sordo.

The *œuvre* of an artist with such varied needs and modes of expression cannot be cut up into chronological slices. It cannot be said, for instance, that between two specific dates Goya was an Expressionist, then a mystical painter, then an ecstatic visionary, then a popular realist, and so on. All his 'periods', to use the conventional term, coexisted in him at all times, developing and manifesting themselves at the most unexpected moments throughout his active career, that is to say, until the day he died.

As for his techniques, these were quite as varied and complex as the motives underlying his artistic aims. A traditionalist painter attached to certain specific methods (even when he revolutionized them, as Delacroix did) could hardly have failed to regard him as a jack of all trades. Everything was grist to his mill, and he used it with diabolical skill and cynicism. In him, each new need for self-expression corresponded to a technique which, even if not new, was so profoundly transformed as to become almost unrecognizable. Goya was essentially 'modern' in his lack of academic prejudice.

The little he said on the subject of his art was compressed into a few words: 'All I see is planes that project and planes that recede, projections and recesses... In Nature, colour does not exist any more than line. Give me a piece of charcoal and I will make you a picture, for the whole of painting is sacrifice and determination.'

From the purely human point of view, Goya's character was neither more nor less complex than that of anyone who is endowed with a body and a soul, who dreams and acts, who is compelled to take account of the past, of the present in which he lives and of the future which he goes to meet as best he may. What was new in Goya was that his empiricism applied to the painter in him as well as the man. Goya's painting was not the fruit of an acquired, perfected and transmissible technique, but a personal adventure recounted as completely as possible by graphic means, just as it might have been recounted through the medium of literary description if Goya had been a writer instead of a painter.

What is fundamentally and, to all appearances, involuntarily 'modern' in Goya's approach is his desire for total self-expression through the medium of a specific form of art (in this case, painting); an art which is originally limited in principle but which tends to universalize itself, to become a genuine language capable of fulfilling the needs of an individual nature which wants to establish contact, through it, with a world from which it feels that it has been cut off. Van Gogh was a prime example of this new type of painter, but Van Gogh's adventure was a conscious one, and his unendurable awareness of it drove him to suicide.

Was Goya aware of his own adventure, or did he only embark on it by chance? We must not forget that until about 1792, when he was past the age of forty, Goya remained a very gifted artist devoid of genuine ambition. He did not become the great painter we know today until he had been afflicted by an illness which left him permanently deaf and unable to communicate with his fellow-beings except through his painting.

Discounting the grandiose illusions of the Romantics and the charming fancies of the Impressionists, he was the first painter to believe, and to demonstrate, that painting could and should be simultaneously *a state of sensation, a state of awareness and a state of mind.*

Let us recall, in conclusion, that Francisco de Goya y Lucientes was born on 30 March 1746 in the Aragonese village of Fuendetodos, whose name means 'fountain of all'.

List of Illustrations

Short Bibliography

Index

List of Illustrations

Figures in italic denote colour reproductions

Short Bibliography

ADHÉMAR, JEAN *Goya*. London, 1948

DELEVOY, ROBERT L. *Goya*. London, 1955

DUMONT, HENRI (intro.) *Goya*. London, 1948

FERRARI, ENRIQUE LAFUENTE (intro.) *Goya : His complete etchings, aquatints and lithographs*. London, 1962

FORMAGGIO, DINO (intro.) *Goya*. London, 1960

HOLLAND, VYVYAN B. *Goya : A Pictorial Biography*. London, 1961

HUXLEY, ALDOUS (intro.) *The Complete Etchings of Goya*. London, 1959

KLINGENDER, FRANCIS D. *Goya in the Democratic Tradition*. London, 1948

LAMBERT, FRANK *Francisco Goya*. London, 1946

MALRAUX, ANDRÉ *Saturn : An Essay on Goya*. London, 1957

MOYNIHAN, RODRIGO *Goya, 1746-1828*. London, 1951

SCHMID, F. *The Technique of Goya*. London, 1942

TOMORY, PETER A. *Goya*. London, 1960

VALLENTIN, ANTONINA *This I Saw : The Life and Times of Goya*. London, 1951

WIGHT, FRED S. (intro.) *Goya, 1746-1828*. London, 1957

The four-volume *catalogue raisonné* by Xavier Desparmet Fitz-Gerald, which includes 447 reproductions of paintings and 34 drawings, was published in Paris in 1950.

Index

The World of Art Library

History of Art

THE ART OF THE ANCIENT NEAR EAST   *Seton Lloyd*
GREEK ART   *John Boardman*
ROMAN ART AND ARCHITECTURE   *Sir Mortimer Wheeler*
ART OF THE EARLY CHRISTIANS   *Michael Gough*
ART OF THE BYZANTINE ERA   *David Talbot Rice*
EARLY MEDIEVAL ART   *John Beckwith*
ART OF CHINA, KOREA AND JAPAN   *Peter Swann*
ISLAMIC ART   *David Talbot Rice*
THE ART OF THE RENAISSANCE   *P. & L. Murray*
LATE RENAISSANCE AND MANNERISM   *P. & L. Murray*
BAROQUE AND ROCOCO   *Germain Bazin*
ART OF THE ROMANTIC ERA   *Marcel Brion*
IMPRESSIONISM   *Phoebe Pool*
PREHISTORIC ART   *T. G. E. Powell*
ANCIENT ARTS OF THE AMERICAS   *G. H. S. Bushnell*
ANCIENT ARTS OF CENTRAL ASIA   *Tamara Talbot Rice*
A CONCISE HISTORY OF ENGLISH PAINTING   *William Gaunt*
A CONCISE HISTORY OF RUSSIAN ART   *Tamara Talbot Rice*
A CONCISE HISTORY OF MODERN PAINTING   *Sir Herbert Read*
EUROPEAN SCULPTURE   *H. D. Molesworth*
A CONCISE HISTORY OF MODERN SCULPTURE   *Sir Herbert Read*

Artists

CHAGALL   *Jean Cassou*
DÜRER   *Marcel Brion*
GAUGUIN   *Georges Boudaille*
VAN GOGH   *Pierre Cabanne*
GOYA   *J.-F. Chabrun*
KLEE   *G. di San Lazzaro*
MICHELANGELO   *Rolf Schott*
HENRY MOORE   *Sir Herbert Read*
PICASSO   *Pierre Daix*
RENOIR   *François Fosca*
SEURAT   *John Russell*
TOULOUSE-LAUTREC   *Jean Bouret*